Saving
The Constitution

From Enemies, Foreign and Domestic

Richard D. Proctor PhD

Published by:
Provis Press
Kaysville, UT
Provis@sulmega.com
801-719-6291

ISBN: 978-0-578-21860-1

Published in the United States of America

Cover by Brian Twede

CONTENTS

Forward

I am the author of a book on the Constitution as well. Even though Richard and I approach the topic differently, Richard's book goes on to explain the Constitution in very plain language that can be easily understood by the young, the old, the higher educated and those with very little education.

Sadly, our Constitution is not well understood, even by those who raise their arms to the square and swear an oath to support and defend it. The reason they get away with it, is that the masses of the People of America are no longer being taught even the basic principles of our Constitution; so the question arises, how does one know when it is being violated if we do not understand or know it? We cannot, any more than, how will we know when one or more of the Ten Commandments are being violated, unless we know them. Well, there is a difference because our consciences tell us that...for the most part.

That being said, Richard's book will help everyone, man, woman or child, to get an important grasp of Constitutional principles so that he/she can hold our Congressmen and women to task and keep the Constitution from being violated. If they know we know and understand Constitutional government, they will think twice before violating it. A great read and very informative.

Lonnie D. Crockett, Ph.D.
Professor of American History

Foundation

This book concerns the Constitution of the United States and to get a full understanding of the document, it is imperative to review the opening statements of The Declaration of Independence. The Declaration of Independence is the foundation of the Constitution and includes our basic God given rights and freedoms.

To this end I have included the first part of that document.

The Declaration of Independence
Action of Second Continental Congress, July 4, 1776

The unanimous Declaration of the thirteen united States of America,

When in the Course of human events, it becomes necessary for one people to dissolve the political bands which have connected them with another, and to assume among the powers of the earth, the separate and equal station to which the Laws of Nature and of Nature's God entitle them, a decent respect to the opinions of mankind requires that they should declare the causes which impel them to the separation.

We hold these truths to be self-evident, that all men are created equal, that they are endowed by their

Creator with certain unalienable Rights, that among these are Life, Liberty and the pursuit of Happiness.-- That to secure these rights, Governments are instituted among Men, deriving their just powers from the consent of the governed, --That whenever any Form of Government becomes destructive of these ends, it is the Right of the People to alter or to abolish it, and to institute new Government, laying its foundation on such principles and organizing its powers in such form, as to them shall seem most likely to effect their Safety and Happiness. Prudence, indeed, will dictate that Governments long established should not be changed for light and transient causes; and accordingly all experience hath shewn, that mankind are more disposed to suffer, while evils are sufferable, than to right themselves by abolishing the forms to which they are accustomed. But when a long train of abuses and usurpations, pursuing invariably the same Object evinces a design to reduce them under absolute Despotism, it is their right, it is their duty, to throw off such Government, and to provide new Guards for their future security.-

Here, clearly stated, are the rights the Creator has given to all people, and the government is tasked to preserve these rights. Ultimately that is the sole purpose of the government and the Constitution was written to outline how these God given rights will be secured.

As such it is imperative for all citizens to fully understand the Constitution, so that they will know what the government is supposed to do. In today's society many of our citizens do not understand what the Constitution requires of the government. Since the people don't understand the

Constitution they have neglected to ensure that the government lives up to its responsibilities. The final purpose of this book is to explain these principles as outlined in the Constitution in an easily understood fashion.

Notice the last words of the quote above: "provide new Guards for their future security." The Constitution provides those guards. It doesn't need to be changed, we just need to follow it as it was originally written.

To ensure that it is followed, we must also consider the effect that the supreme court is having on our lives. In 1803 John James Marshall decided in the case Marbury v Madison that the supreme court has the authority to decide on the constitutionality of laws passed by the Congress and signed by the President. This has been further expanded to include the legality of almost anything that the federal government does. This power has also been expanded to include the amendments to the Constitution.

As this unconstitutional tradition continued throughout the history of the United States, the federal courts got involved in such minutia as how the State of Florida counted its votes for President. This tradition is completely out of control. The supreme court and the other federal courts dip their fingers into every item the state and federal government gets involved in.

On the 28th of September in 1820 in a letter to William C. Jarvis, Thomas Jefferson stated in part.

"Our judges are as honest as other men, and not more so. They have, with others, the same passions for party, for power, and the privilege of their corps;

and their power is the more dangerous as they are in office for life, and not responsible, as the other functionaries are, to the elective control...

"When the legislative or executive functionaries act unconstitutionally, they are responsible to the people in their elective capacity. The exemption of judges from that [i.e., from elections] is quite dangerous enough. I know of no safe depository of the ultimate powers of the society but the people themselves; and if we think them not enlightened enough to exercise their control with a wholesome discretion, the remedy is not to take it from them, but to inform their discretion by education.

"...If the three powers maintain their mutual independence of each other, the government may last long, but not so if either can assume the authorities of the other." (Bergh, The Writings of Thomas Jefferson, vol. 15, pages 277-278)

Also in Volume 5 of *The Founders' Constitution*, page 364 Thomas Jefferson is quoted as saying:

"It is better to leave a cause to the decision of cross and pile, than to that of a judge biassed to one side; and that the opinion of 12 honest jurymen gives still a better hope of right, than cross and pile does. It is left therefore to the juries, if they think the permanent judges are under any biass whatever in any cause, to take upon themselves to judge the law as well as the fact. Thomas Jefferson on 19 July 1789, Papers 15:282-83

Therefore, in the eyes of Thomas Jefferson and according to Article III of the Constitution the supreme court has no judicial authority decide anything on most of these cases it reviews.

A significant indication of this bias and inability of the supreme court to maintain a constant direction has to do with direct taxes on the citizens of the United States. In Springer v United States (1880) the court found that direct taxes were unconstitutional as they were not apportioned properly. Again in Pollock v. Farmers' Loan and Trust Company (1895) the Court ruled that the unapportioned income tax on income from land was unconstitutional.

Here we have two separate supreme court decisions that set a precedence that unapportioned taxes on the incomes of the people was unconstitutional.

Then in 1916 in spite of the previous supreme court decisions and the actual words in the Constitution the court decided that income taxes were constitutional no matter what the Constitution said.

This is exactly what Jefferson warned us about. The court's decisions are based on whatever the whims of its members and the current government want at the time. As you read this book you will find one item after another where the federal government has overstepped its authority and we have allowed it by our quiet acceptance. We must take control of our states and nullify every action from the federal government that is not in accordance with the Constitution as ratified in 1788. That includes any amendments to the Constitution, any laws passed by Congress, any federal court decisions, any executive orders, and any agency rules that are not in accordance with the original Constitution.

Introduction

The goal of this book is to go over the Constitution one paragraph at a time. The original meaning of many of the phrases, ideas, and requirements of the Constitution have been lost over time, and our education system no longer teaches anything about the actual Constitution. Most courses spend more time on the history of the Constitution than on the actual document itself. The People, who are one of the powers that created the Constitution, do not read or understand what it says. This book is intended to help correct that oversight by explaining the Constitution in plain contemporary language. I will endeavor to explain the paragraphs and discuss their meanings and intentions. The Constitution is not really hard to read, but we don't take time to do it.

The Constitution has only 4,694 words and was written on one piece of parchment, so each word and punctuation mark was very important. They did not include any word that was not necessary. So, when we read the document, each word must be considered. A word such as "or" indicates there is another thought. A word such as "and" means the following is included with the previous concept. A phrase such as "the judicial power shall" would indicate a precise intention.

The total word count of the amendments is 3,337, and these amendments are officially considered part of the document. This total number of words, if written in an average book, would be only a short pamphlet of around 30 pages. That is not a huge undertaking, yet as a people we don't take the time out to read it. This is a significant error on our part.

As I explain the Constitution, I will repeatedly use *Webster's Dictionary of 1928*, *The Founders' Constitution* Volumes 1 through 5, and The Heritage Guide to the Constitution. Care will be taken in using the Heritage Guide, as it mostly follows case law and precedents that the supreme court has established. This case law and the precedents have changed the Constitution to whatever the judges and the federal government wanted it to be, at the time.

Abraham Lincoln warned: "Don't interfere with anything in the Constitution. That must be maintained, for it is the only safeguard of our liberties." Despite those words of wisdom, today's court jesters have constantly interfered with the First Amendment, which perhaps contains the most significant 46 words in the history of civilization. They have used these words to legalize pornography and flag burning while denouncing Christmas, God, the Boy Scouts, and prayer. None of these actions are justified by the Constitution. The supreme court will not allow the Ten Commandments to be posted in American courtrooms or any public building, even though they are on the wall of the court itself.

My comments, explaining the Constitution, are written in larger print to allow the reader to easily identify the explanations. The Constitution is the most important part of this book, but I felt that the explanations needed to be easily seen and separated.

I am sure that I will miss some concepts or make some mistakes, and I welcome constructive comments so that this book can be the best possible to enhance our citizen's overall knowledge of the most important document of this the United States of America.

I would like to begin this book with some general comments concerning several items of the Constitution that have had a significant affect on our lives.

supreme court

As you may notice I never capitalize the supreme court. The word supreme is only included seven times in the Constitution and it is never capitalized. The term indicates a hierarchy between the federal supreme court and the federal inferior courts and neither has authority over the State courts.

Liberty, Freedom and Power

Let's take a moment and review the concepts of liberty, freedom, and power. First, what is freedom vs. liberty? Liberty is freedom with responsibility. The best way to describe freedom could be that we are free to do anything we want as long as it doesn't violate the freedom of anyone else. That means you can do anything you want, but you must accept the consequences of your decisions. Liberty is a higher principle than freedom.

What is power? Power is the concept of force. One individual forces another to do what he wants. Force removes freedom and liberty. Government is force, but government is necessary to allow us to live around everybody else. Government provides an orderly society with laws to assist us in our interaction with others. The Constitution was written to limit the force of government and still provide an orderly and secure environment.

3

Separate But Equal

We have all heard the term "separate but equal." The word separate is never found in the Constitution. Usually this phrase refers to the three branches of the government, but that is not correct. There is a hierarchy within the three branches of government and the Constitution establishes that order. The first and most important branch is the Congressional Branch outlined in Article I which is the longest article. Then within the Congress the House of Representatives is more important than the Senate as the House represents the People. The Executive Branch is the next in line with the judiciary following and is the least important. Today because of power grabbing, that sequence is almost reversed as the supreme court has set itself above every other government within the entire country. Today, the supreme court could be referred to as the Nine Emperors. Separate but equal is an artificial phrase that has developed over time.

Freedoms and Rights

What are specific freedoms mentioned in the Constitution? There are four, and they are all included in the First Amendment. They are freedom of religion, freedom to exercise the requirements of that religion, freedom of speech and freedom of the press.

What are the rights established by the Constitution? There are twenty-seven rights specifically mentioned as follows:

- There are two in the First Amendment: the right to assemble and the right to petition the government.
- The Second Amendment contains two rights: 1. the right to keep arms and 2. the right to bear arms.
- The Third Amendment contains two rights: the right to not provide housing for soldiers 1. during peace time and 2. during war
- The Fourth Amendment contains four rights establishing: 1. the right to be secure in our homes, 2. the right against unreasonable searches and seizures, 3. the right protecting citizens from improper warrants, and 4. The right that a warrant must describe particularly the place to be searched and the persons or things to be seized.
- The Fifth Amendment contains five separate rights: 1. The right to a Grand Jury, 2. the right protecting us from being tried for the same item twice, 3. the right to not be required to witness against himself, 4. The right of life, liberty and property, and 5. the right that property cannot be taken without proper compensation. This is the only time private property is actually mentioned in the Constitution.
- The Sixth Amendment has six separate rights to do with trials: 1. the right to a speedy and public trial; 2. the right for an impartial jury; 3. the right to be informed of the nature of the accusation; 4. the right to be confronted by the witnesses against him; 5. the right to compel witnesses for him; and 6. the right to counsel for his defense.
- The Seventh Amendment establishes the right to a trial by jury in civil cases and the right that civil cases will remain civil cases in all US courts.

- The Eighth Amendment contains 3 rights: 1. the right establishing that no excessive bail can to required; 2. no excessive fines shall be imposed; and 3. no cruel or unusual punishments shall be inflicted.
- The Ninth Amendment establishes an inclusive right stating additional rights not included in the previous amendments shall not be denied.
- The last listed right in the amendments is the right to vote. It is included 5 times under different conditions. These are in Amendments 14, 15, 19, 24 and 26.

Early Violations of the Constitution

The Constitution was ratified in 1788 and by 1824 there were already 10 significant violations of it principles. These violations occurred while the Founding Fathers and their immediate children were still alive.

1. In 1790, the number of legislators was increased from the constitutional number of 30,000 people per representative to 56, 945.

Even as early as 1790, Article I, Section 2, Paragraph 3, which states "The number of Representatives shall not exceed one for every thirty Thousand" was ignored because each representative represented around 56,945 individuals. The population of the United States was around 3,929,214 which according to the Constitution should have resulted in 131 representatives. During the entire period of the Constitutional Convention, the delegates regularly discussed how many people each representative should represent. The number 50,000 was rejected and during the last few days of the

Convention it was determined that 30,000 should be the number.

With the census of 1790, the government ignored the Constitution and set the number arbitrarily at around 50,000. That number provided the larger States with more power in the federal government, which had been the goal of the Federalists right from the beginning.

Looking at the actual number of legislators during the first five decades of the Republic, each representative was representing from 50,000 to 60,000 people. After the Civil War, the number of individuals per representative grew every decade until the 1920s. Based on the 1920 census, the number of representatives should have been at least 3,534. Why do you think that the number was capped at only 435 or 12% of the Constitution's requirement? Think about who gained the most power when this change was instituted.

Today there are nearly 800,000 people represented by each legislator.

2. In 1791, the first central bank officially began. The Constitution states in Article I, Section 8, Paragraph 5 that the Congress is to "To coin Money, regulate the Value thereof." In 1791 the Congress gave that power to a central bank and that began the control of our country by the International Banking Establishment. These individuals are European financiers and through our Central Bank, The Federal Reserve, they are actually controlling the value of our money and our government. See my volumes in the *Liberty: Will it survive the 21st Century?* series.

The value of money is regulated by the amount of money in existence. More money creates inflation. A shortage of money creates recessions or depressions. Business cycles are a reflection of ups and downs in the money supply. Thus whenever the International Banking Establishment wanted the United States in a depression or recession, they just reduced the money supply to cause it. That was the cause of the Great Depression of the 1930s, less money in circulation. The power to control the money supply should never be given to a private company or a foreign entity and the Federal Reserve is both a private company and a company completely controlled by foreigners.

3. In 1796, the supreme court decided to misinterpret Article VI and decided that treaties were over and more important than the Constitution. They created a new supreme law of the land based on treaties.

4. In 1800, the political party system completely replaced the requirements of the Constitution as outlined in Article II Section 1, Paragraph 2. Because of the political parties, the Electoral College has never functioned after the election in the year 1800. Our elections have become a circus rather than a selection of a statesman to govern our country.

5. In 1803, John J. Marshall decided that the supreme court needed more power and used the term judicial review to provide the supreme court with more governmental power than the Congress and the President.

Here we have a small group of men and women, sitting on the supreme court, who have set themselves up as superior to the rest of us. They have assumed they can change the Constitution whenever they decide and in whatever manner they decide. They override anything and everything that the original Founders achieved whenever it suits them, and we quietly allow it.

Now educators, teaching the Constitution, commonly ignore the original document and teach whatever the supreme court has decided. The courts now pass laws and control our entire culture. Almost every decision of the supreme court is either out of their jurisdiction or completely unconstitutional. They have destroyed the values and the fabric of our nation. This will be discussed in detail during the discussion of Article III and has been thoroughly covered in my *Liberty Will it Survive* series of six volumes.

6.   In 1804, the Twelfth Amendment continued the gutting of the Electoral process.

7.   In 1808, the agreement reached during the Constitutional Convention regarding slavery was ignored and slavery was continued. This was done in spite of the agreements that were required to get the Constitution signed and ratified. Since we did not eliminate slavery in a civilized manner, a devastating war was the result.

8. In 1816, Marshall continued his drive for more power and the illegal position of emperor of the United States by taking over the state's laws and constitutions. Here we have a Justice destroying one of the powers that actually formed the federal government. His ego had no bounds. It was not the Civil War but this decision that destroyed the States sovereignty.

9. In 1819, Marshall decided that he got his power from the people and took another big step toward the destruction of the Republic.

10. Finally in 1824, the supreme court changed the simple meaning of Article I, Section 8, Paragraph 3: "To regulate Commerce with foreign Nations, and among the several States, and with the Indian tribes." Originally the commerce clause established by the Constitution regulated the trade between the States, foreign countries and the Indians. Marshall began the path to make interstate commerce a function that now controls our lives and destroys our liberties by even regulating what we can grow in our own backyard for our own use.

These ten items have changed our liberty loving country into a central government that cannot satisfy itself. Every day some other part of this federal government behemoth finds a new way to destroy our liberties. We must learn our Constitution and then hold our government to it.

Oath of office, enlistment, or commissioning

A question arises about the oath of office taken by all military individuals. Does that oath expire? Many individuals have asked that question. Here is a common answer to that question.

Your Oath of Enlistment or Commissioning is not enforceable in and of itself. (Can you imagine what would happen if politicians could be held accountable to their oaths which have similar declarations?) It is merely a declaration that you voluntarily submit yourself to the provisions of the Uniform Code of Military Justice (UCMJ) so long as you serve. Technically, you remain obligated to that service until discharged.

Morally and ethically, many veterans consider themselves bound by their promise to support and defend the Constitution against all enemies, foreign and domestic, for life. However, that is a personal choice, an honorable choice, the choice of a citizen who recognizes that America is not defined by a land mass, but rather by principles codified in the Constitution. We may pledge allegiance to symbols of the Republic, but in actuality, without the Constitution and dedicated observance of it, there is no nation. It seems that service members and veterans understand this better than most. Sadly, the sum total of those who serve or have served is a scant minority of the nation and the proportion of those who have not learned these same lessons are growing exponentially with every passing generation.

I consider myself under obligation for life to the Constitution as it was originally intended.

Richard Proctor

Overview

The Constitution is an amazing document. It has lasted as a government document longer than any other government document in the entire history of the World. It is like the Ten Commandments. They were recorded when Moses received them ON Mount Sinai and have lasted for more than 30 centuries. They are still as important today as they were on the first day.

The Constitution is the same kind of document. It is as relevant today as it was in 1788 when it was ratified. It is astounding to me that many think that it must be updated. It is a document of how a government should operate with regard to its people. In the eyes of God, the people have freedom and free agency. The Constitution was established to create a system of government that would tie the government down to its main responsibility. That responsibility is to provide an environment of safety, where the people could operate with confidence in spite of man's basic desire to control other people.

It was written in seven parts or articles. Article I, establishes the branch of the government that creates the laws. It also covers how the laws should be established and what the federal government and the state governments can and cannot do. Article II establishes the branch of government that is responsible for executing the laws and the administration of the government. It covers how the Presidency should operate including how the president is elected and what he has authority to do. Article III establishes the federal judiciary. Article IV establishes how additional states could be added and their basic operations. Article V establishes how to amend the Constitution when it is necessary. Article VI establishes what laws are supreme throughout the nation. Article VII establishes how to ratify the Constitution or in other words how it would be accepted by the people and the states that were the two powers of its creation.

Then each section within each article treats different subjects. In Article I there are ten sections.

- Section 1 decrees who makes the laws.
- Section 2 covers the selection of the people's representatives.
- Section 3 covers the selection of the state's representatives. It must be understood that the two powers that created the document were the states and the people. That is what is meant by the separation of powers, the people's power and the states' power. Neither wanted to give this new federal government the ability to control them. It is similar to two parents having a child. The parents are in charge and the child obeys them. Therefore, the people and the states are in charge and the federal government obeys them.
- Section 4 establishes how to select these two sets of representatives.
- Section 5 covers how each House, referring to both the House of Representatives and the Senate, should operate.
- Section 6 establishes how they would be compensated for their service.
- Section 7 sets up how each part would interact with the other.

- Section 8 sets down the powers that this new government would have. The powers are listed precisely and no others are allowed.
- Section 9 outlines how new people are to be allowed to be a part of the nation and how they will function within the nation.
- Section 10 establishes the limits on how states would operate with regards to the other states.

There are four sections in Article II.

- Section 1 establishes the terms of the president or CEO and the vice president of this new government. It outlines precisely how that these individuals are to be elected. Since this new government is a Republic the people select other people or representatives to make the selections and then presents these selections to the Congress established in Article one to make the final decisions.
- Section 2 provides for the limited power of the president.
- Section 3 establishes how the president will operate with the Congress.
- Section 4 covers how the president will be removed from office if there is a need to do so.

Article III has three sections establishing precise limits of the judicial functions of the new government. Judges are necessary in cases when the laws of the federal government are broken.

- Section 1 establishes the limits of the judicial power of these federal judges.
- Section 2 outlines precisely the areas of authority of these federal judges. Remember that these judges are to adjudicate only the laws of the federal government.
- Section 3 establishes the protections for the people.

Article IV has four sections.

- Section 1 is about the records of the states.
- Section 2 is again protection for the people.
- Section 3 is how to admit new states.
- Section 4 guarantees the type of government within each state.

Article V has one paragraph and that covers how to amend or add to the Constitution.

Article VI has four paragraphs which establishes the supreme law of the nation.

Article VII has two paragrsphs covering the ratification of the Constitution itself.

Finally, there are the signatures of the creators of this document and the states they represented.

That completes the basic overview of the document. Now we can go right to the document and discuss what it means paragraph by paragraph.

An item of importance is the name of the document. Originally it did not have a title. The last eight words of the preamble contain the real title of the document. These words are: "This Constitution for the United States of America." The name cannot be The Constitution of the United States of America as there was no United States of America on the date the document was completed. The United States didn't exist until the Constitution was finally ratified on June 21, 1788.

Look at those eight words again at the end of the Preamble: "This Constitution for the United States of America." This really means, this document is for the current 13 states or entities or individual governments that are located in America to become united. The change of the name of the Constitution to what we have today occurred in 1871 in an act of Congress. For a complete discussion of the effect of this change see my book *Liberty: Will it Survive the 21st Century?* Vol 2 pages 9 to 15. You will be surprised at what occurred in 1871 as it has been hidden very well.

The Constitution

Preamble

We the People of the United States, in Order to form a more perfect Union, establish Justice, insure domestic Tranquility, provide for the common defense, promote the general Welfare, and secure the Blessings of Liberty to ourselves and our Posterity, do ordain and establish this Constitution for the United States of America.

Here we have the introduction to the Constitution. The last line establishes that this document is for the States or entities that existed in the geographical area that was to become the nation that would eventually be called the United States of America. There was no United States of America prior to the ratification of this document. There was no title over the original document. The closest thing to a title is the last line.

The people wanted to create a government with the following attributes: "to form a more perfect Union, establish Justice, insure domestic Tranquility, provide for the common defense, promote the general Welfare, and secure the Blessings of Liberty to ourselves and our Posterity." This statement was the reason for the contract. Notice the word welfare

19

is defined as general Welfare which denotes a welfare for all of the people not specific individuals. This was preceded by the words establish Justice and insure domestic Tranquility. The nation was formed to provide these conditions, so that the people would have a safe and secure environment for transacting business and living their lives. The phrase in between these two is to provide for the common defense. This common defense was to ensure that the nation would be secure from foreign powers. It included secure established borders to allow for the nation to develop and thrive without foreigners invading and destroying us. A definition of invading would include armies as well as groups of people with evil intentions.

Let's spend a minute on the welfare clause, "promote the general Welfare." There are only two instances of the word welfare included in the Constitution. The first is in the Preamble as we have noticed. The second is in Article I, Section 8, Paragraph 1 and it says:

> "The Congress shall have Power To lay and collect Taxes, Duties, Imposts and Excises, to pay the Debts and provide for the common Defense and general Welfare of the United States; but all Duties, Imposts and

Excises shall be uniform throughout the United States;

Note the phrase in the Preamble, "provide for the common defense, promote the general Welfare." And then the phrase in Article I, "provide for the common Defense and general Welfare of the United States."

In both cases it states, "provide for the common defense," but the words about welfare are very different. The word "promote" in the Preamble, and the word "provide" in Article I. Promote and provide are very important. First it says promote the general Welfare. Promote doesn't say provide and general welfare means for all the people. Then in the second reference it says provide for the general Welfare of the United States which is also for all of the people. Therefore, the Constitution declares that we promote the general welfare by providing for the general welfare of the people not the individual. This is not about handouts or giving people money or goods or anything. This is about providing an atmosphere of tranquil conditions within the nation so that the citizens can prosper.

During the time of the Founders the word "welfare," meant, faring well, or having an atmosphere of peace and order and the purpose of the government was to allow everyone to live in that type of atmosphere.

The supreme court has found rights where none existed and those rights now take billions of dollars from the working classes and give it to the idle in the form of social caring. We take care of the idle by stealing from the worker.

The first part of the Preamble stated the goals of the Constitution, and the second was the reason for these goals. The reason was to secure the Blessings of Liberty to ourselves and our Posterity. This simply means that the Founders knew that they needed and wanted a government that would provide protections that would encourage liberty. This liberty would then allow the citizens to live and work without interference from foes within the country or outside of it.

In the 1828 dictionary welfare is defined as:
1. Exemption from misfortune, sickness, calamity or evil; the enjoyment of health and the common blessings of life; prosperity; happiness; applied to persons.

2. Exemption from any unusual evil or calamity; the enjoyment of peace and prosperity, or the ordinary blessings of society and civil government; applied to states.

Article I

The Legislative Branch

Article I, Section 1

Section 1. All legislative Powers herein granted shall be vested in a Congress of the United States, which shall consist of a Senate and House of Representatives.

The first sentence of the Constitution defines who can make the laws of the country. It says the legislature is the only body that can make laws. It doesn't say that when the mood takes them, the president or the supreme court could make the laws. It doesn't say that if the president wants, he can write executive orders that will be treated as laws. It doesn't say that opinions of the supreme court are laws. It says only the legislature can make laws. Quite clear isn't it? But look at what has happened as the other branches of government have decided they wanted more power than the contract allows them. And we the people accepted these changes as laws, so it has become a tradition for these government departments to make laws. All of these numerous laws are in fact illegal because the Constitution is the supreme law of the land and it states that only the Legislature can make laws.

Article I, Section 2, Paragraph 1

Section 2. The House of Representatives shall be composed of Members chosen every second Year by the People of the several States, and the Electors in each State shall have the Qualifications requisite for Electors of the most numerous Branch of the State Legislature.

The first and most important body created by the Constitution is the House of Representatives because it represents the people. Here the term of office is specified and who selects these individuals.

The last phrase of the paragraph is very difficult to understand. Here is an explanation provided by the Heritage Guide to the Constitution.

"At the Constitutional Convention, the Framers debated whether the electors of the House of Representative should be limited to freeholders, or whether they should incorporate state voting laws by requiring that whoever the state decided is eligible to vote for "the most numerous Branch of the State Legislature" is also eligible to vote for the House of Representatives. The majority of the delegates preferred to defer to the states and approved the Elector Qualifications Clause.

As James Wilson summarized in records of the Convention, "It was difficult to form any uniform rule of qualifications for all the States. Unnecessary innovations, he thought, should also be avoided: "It would be very hard & disagreeable for the same persons, at the same time, to vote for representatives in the State Legislature and to be excluded from a vote for those in the Natl. Legislature."

"Thus, the Constitution gives authority for determining elector qualifications to the states. The Seventeenth Amendment adopted the same qualifications language to apply to the popular election of United States Senators.

That is the best explanation of this paragraph, and it simply means that anyone who could vote for candidates in the State could also vote for candidates in the national election.

Article I, Section 2, Paragraph 2

> **No Person shall be a Representative who shall not have attained to the Age of twenty five Years, and been seven Years a Citizen of the United States, and who shall not, when elected, be an Inhabitant of that State in which he shall be chosen.**

These are the requirements to be eligible to run for office as a representative in the House of Representatives. These requirements are precise and clear when you keep track of all of the negative words. So far these requirements have not been violated.

Article I, Section 2, Paragraph 3

Representatives and direct Taxes shall be apportioned among the several States which may be included within this Union, according to their respective Numbers, which shall be determined by adding to the whole Number of free Persons, including those bound to Service for a Term of Years, and excluding Indians not taxed, three fifths of all other Persons. The actual Enumeration shall be made within three Years after the first Meeting of the Congress of the United States, and within every subsequent Term of ten Years, in such Manner as they shall by Law direct. The number of Representatives shall not exceed one for every thirty Thousand, but each State shall have at Least one Representative; and until such enumeration shall be made, the State of New Hampshire shall be entitled to choose three, Massachusetts eight, Rhode Island and Providence Plantations one, Connecticut five, New York six, New Jersey four, Pennsylvania eight, Delaware one, Maryland six,

Virginia ten, North Carolina five, South Carolina five, and Georgia three.

The first line in this paragraph is very significant as it establishes that direct taxes must be apportioned based on population. The removal of the phrase "and direct Taxes" by the Fourteenth Amendment was a very serious change. It was the first of several steps to require direct income taxes on the people. These steps were concluded by the Sixteenth Amendment in 1913 and the supreme court decision in 1916.

Another item overlooked in this first line is that "direct Taxes shall be apportioned among the several States." This is very clear and means that the federal government, when it needs money, is to tax the States directly, NOT the people. The people are a part of the State tax base. The federal government was supposed to keep its hands off the people.

The next part of this paragraph determines how the official population of the State is to be determined. Today, without the benefit of knowing what was going on in the late 1700s, many have taken issue with the 3/5 value for the slaves. The entire issue of slavery was a major problem throughout the entire Convention. Also, these men were honest men with great characters. They did not want slavery in the new nation.

We had just won the Revolutionary War, and they did not want to give the South back to England. Here is the financial problem they faced. The plantations in the South had been financed by the European banks, especially the Bank of England. Much of the collateral behind the loans that established the plantations was based on the value of the slaves. If the slaves were freed, that value would be lost, and the Bank of England could confiscate these plantations. That had to be prevented. The delegates found a compromise. They agreed to begin the ending of slavery in 20 years or by 1808. (We will see this date in Article I, Section 9 and in Article V.) The delegates felt that by then they would be able to get their plantations out from under the Bank of England.

But that wasn't the only problem. The method of counting the slaves without upsetting the balance of power among the states was significant. The slaves outnumbered the slave owners by quite a large margin and since, at the time, slaves could not vote but their numbers were counted along with the slave owners to go towards the decision of the number of representatives. Each state could have the number of representatives based on population, the number of representatives would be unfairly proportioned, giving slave states more representatives in the Congress than the non-slave states. Basically if the slaves were counted like everybody else, the Southern States would have greater power than the Northern States in the new government.

The 3/5 rule was the compromise that allowed the Constitution to go forward. Without that compromise the Constitution would never have been signed. If the slave states had just kept to the 1808 agreement, all of the slavery problems during the middle of the 1800s would not have occurred.

Then the determination of when to begin the enumeration or census of the population of the States was agreed upon, along with how often.

The next sticky point was how to determine how many representatives each state would have. This discussion was also linked to the number of Senators because the smaller States might not have the same representation as the larger States. If the number of people per representative was large then the smaller States would have proportionally fewer representatives. This issue was debated throughout all the weeks of the Convention.

We must take a look at the makeup of the delegates who were at the Convention, because that makeup would determine whether the smaller States had more power than the larger States. There was a distinctive difference in the political views of two vying groups. One point of view was a concern of the larger states. These were men who wanted a strong central government. They saw the major fallacy of the Articles of Confederation. That fallacy was that the federal government could do nothing because all of the States could not work together. Those who wanted a strong central government came to be known as the Federalists. The other group were those who wanted to preserve the autonomy and power of the individual States by forming a weaker central government. They came to be known as the Anti-Federalists. Both of these factions wanted the Constitution but under different rules.

These two factions could not come to a satisfactory agreement as to how many people each representative should represent. The debate on this issue went on during the entire Convention. The smaller States, Anti-Federalists, did not want the larger states to dominate the government. The smaller States wanted to be represented. The larger States, Federalists, did not want to give the smaller States too much power. This controversy was another area that also almost terminated the Convention.

The final agreement on the number of representatives was finally agreed during the last days of the Convention. It was suggested that each representative would represent 30,000 people with each State having at least one representative. Finally, a number was suggested that was small enough to satisfy the smaller States and large enough to satisfy the larger States.

This provision was violated within two years of the ratification of the Constitution by immediately using the number of 50,000 people per representative, which limited the number of representatives for the smaller States. Today, without an amendment to the Constitution, that number has increased to over 700,000 people per representative and is still growing. In our day the problem of the larger States dominating the smaller States has become apparent. The smaller States are even called fly-over States meaning we don't need to bother with them. If we used the 30,000 number for representation there would be no fly-over States.

This number of how many representatives each State would have also affects the Electoral College as we will discuss in Article II.

If we had held to the number of 30,000 people per representative today we would have in excess of 10,000 representatives in the House of Representatives. Many consider that this number would be too large to handle. But think about these ideas.

- First, for the special interest groups to control the Congress would be much more difficult than it is because the majority would be in excess of 5,000. It is hard to influence 5,000 people.
- Second, the representatives could be required to live in their districts rather than in Washington, D.C. so the people could more easily keep in touch with them.
- Third, the computer systems that exist today would make it easy to communicate with video and phone connections.
- Fourth, there could be a requirement that all funds raised for campaigning must come from the people in the district. As there would only be 30,000 people the representatives could more easily speak with all of them on a regular basis.

All of these items would create a more responsive political situation.

Article I, Section 2, Paragraph 4

When vacancies happen in the Representation from any State, the Executive Authority thereof shall issue Writs of Election to fill such Vacancies.

In this paragraph the procedures for the States to fill the vacancies were agreed upon. The executive authority refers to the State governments who would have this responsibility.

Article I, Section 2, Paragraph 5

The House of Representatives shall chuse their Speaker and other Officers, and shall have the sole Power of Impeachment.

These are the governing agreements within the House of Representatives itself. This paragraph assigns the power of impeachment to the House. The Senate was assigned the responsibility of the court proceedings whenever the House impeached anyone.

Article I, Section 3, Paragraph 1

Section 3. The Senate of the United States shall be composed of two Senators from each State, chosen by the legislature thereof, for six Years; and each Senator shall have one Vote.

This is a very clear section on how the Senators would be chosen. The Senators are the representatives of the States. As already mentioned, there were two powers that created the new government, the People and the States. The people's representatives became The House of Representatives and the State's representatives became the Senate.

A little known or understood responsibility of the Senator's representation of the States, is the control of the spending of the government. A major reason for the States to have the Senators represent them was because they were responsible for any extra spending by the government. According to Article I, Section 2, Paragraph 3, some of the taxes authorized by the Convention are direct taxes on the States. When the citizens decided that the government should do something for them, they would go to their representatives and ask them to get it for them. So, to satisfy their constituents, they would prepare a bill asking for these items.

All bills for spending originate in the House. When that bill was forwarded to the Senate after passing the House of Representatives one of the considerations of the Senate would be the cost of the requested items. The Senators would evaluate this cost and see if the cost would be passed on to the

States for payment. They also wanted to keep their positions, so they would not approve additional spending. The representatives would go back to the citizens and report that they tried to get it for them and blame the Senate. In this way, the budget could be kept under control.

A major item of the Constitution was the power of the Senate. This had to be changed. To accomplish this the Seventeenth Amendment was created, giving the power of the Senate to the people. Now, the States lost their representation and there was no budget control. We can easily see what has happened to the control of the spending of the federal government.

Article I, Section 3, Paragraph 2

> **Immediately after they shall be assembled in Consequence of the first Election, they shall be divided as equally as may be into three Classes. The Seats of the Senators of the first Class shall be vacated at the Expiration of the second Year, of the second Class at the Expiration of the fourth Year, and of the third Class at the Expiration of the sixth Year, so that one third may be chosen every second Year; and if Vacancies happen by Resignation, or otherwise, during the Recess of the Legislature of any State, the Executive thereof may make temporary Appointments until the next Meeting of the Legislature, which shall then fill such Vacancies.**

This is the paragraph that begins the overlapping of the Senators so that 1/3 will be selected every two years. That would keep some continuity in the Senate. The procedures were also established to fill any vacancies that occurred.

Article I, Section 3, Paragraph 3

No Person shall be a Senator who shall not have attained to the Age of thirty Years, and been nine Years a Citizen of the United States, and who shall not, when elected, be an Inhabitant of that State for which he shall be chosen.

The qualifications to be a Senator are listed here. An important item in this paragraph is that a Senator must be an inhabitant of the State he represents.

Article I, Section 3, Paragraph 4

The Vice President of the United States shall be President of the Senate, but shall have no Vote unless they be equally divided.

This paragraph established the organization of the Senate and gave the Executive Branch some influence and power in the Senate.

Article I, Section 3, Paragraph 5

The Senate shall chuse their other Officers, and also a President pro tempore, in the Absence of the Vice President, or when he shall exercise the Office of President of the United States.

This paragraph gave the Senators the power to organize themselves and to establish rules in case the Vice-President was not available.

Let's stop and consider one of the rules the Senate has adopted. A procedure was established in the Senate that provided for a 60 vote rule. What is this 60 vote rule? Some say that that was the intent of the Founders. What garbage!

Here is a summary of the 60 vote rule and the effect of it. The Senate has been fooling around with ways to control the power in the Senate ever since the Seventeenth Amendment. When that amendment was passed it skewed the whole purpose of the Senate. The Senate was established to give the States power. Now the political forces criticized the Constitution because in the Senate the small States have more power per person that the larger States. This whole debate is topsy-turvy.

Then because of this debacle, special rules were established in the Senate to try to fix the problem. First there was a 2/3 rule. Then the 60 vote rule was established. All of this was to get the power of the people in the Senate balanced. BUT THE PEOPLE SHOULD HAVE NO POWER IN THE SENATE! That is very clear in the original Constitution which is the contract established between the People and the States establishing the federal government. As we will discuss again, Black's Law Dictionary very clearly states that an amendment cannot change a contract. The contract, titled the Constitution, has been illegally altered and thus all of these problems occurred. The Seventeenth Amendment is and always has been unconstitutional and illegal both by law and by the contract itself.

Article I, Section 3, Paragraph 6

> **The Senate shall have the sole Power to try all Impeachments. When sitting for that Purpose, they shall be on Oath or Affirmation. When the President of the United States is tried, the Chief Justice shall preside: and no Person shall be convicted without the Concurrence of two thirds of the Members present.**

Here are the procedures of impeachment of federal government officials. Note that 2/3 of members present are required for impeachment and that the Chief Justice of the supreme court presides at the impeachment of the president.

There is also a specific requirement for the Senators to be "on Oath or Affirmation." Why is the word "or" used? Here are the definitions from *Webster's Dictionary of 1828*:

"Oath: A solemn affirmation or declaration, made with an appeal to God for the truth of what is affirmed. The appeal to God in an oath implies that the person imprecates his vengeance and renounces his favor if the declaration is false, or if the declaration is a promise, the person invokes the vengeance of God if he should fail to fulfill it. A false *oath* is called perjury.

"Affirmation: 4. A solemn declaration made under the penalties of perjury, by persons who conscientiously decline taking an oath; which *affirmation* is in law equivalent to testimony given under oath.

The "or" in this case provides for the situation when a person objects to taking an Oath. An affirmation serves the same purpose as an Oath. All anticipated circumstances were provided for by having two options.

39

Article I, Section 3, Paragraph 7

> **Judgment in Cases of Impeachment shall not extend further than to removal from Office, and disqualification to hold and enjoy any Office of honor, Trust, or Profit under the United States: but the Party convicted shall nevertheless be liable and subject to Indictment, Trial, Judgment and Punishment, according to Law.**

Punishments handed down by Congress are no more than removal from office But if there is cause, the individual can be tried in court for the offense.

Article I, Section 4, Paragraph 1

> **Section 4. The Times, Places and Manner of holding Elections for Senators and Representative,s shall be prescribed in each State by the Legislature thereof; but the Congress may at any time by Law make or alter such Regulations, except as to the Places of chusing Senators.**

In this section the general regulations of selecting Senators and Representatives are established, including giving Congress the power to alter those rules with regard to the House of Representatives. It also very clearly states that the regulations regarding the locations of the election of the Senators is not within the power of the Congress.

This is another item in the Constitution indicating that the Senators are under the control of the States.

Article I, Section 4, Paragraph 2

The Congress shall assemble at least once in every Year, and such Meeting shall be on the first Monday in December, unless they shall by Law appoint a different Day.

Interesting that it is indicated that the Founders did not see the Congress as having long sessions. They felt it should be in December which is the time of the year that many regular occupations were reduced based on the weather. They probably felt that a few days in December would be sufficient to transact normal business.

Article I, Section 5, Paragraph 1

Section 5. Each House shall be the judge of the Elections, Returns and Qualifications of its own Members, and a Majority of each shall constitute a Quorum to do Business; but a smaller Number may adjourn from day to day, and may be authorized to compel the Attendance of absent Members, in such Manner and under such Penalties as each House may provide.

Here we find some administrative rules concerning the members of the Houses of Congress. These rules include the statement that a majority of the membership is required to constitute a quorum and that quorum can do business. As we will see in Article II, Section 1, Paragraph 3, a quorum will consist of two thirds of the States when electing the President. Then in Section 3, Paragraph 6, of Article I, we see that 2/3 of the members present are required to impeach a President. In all other business this section prevails.

This paragraph also allows the compulsion of absent members and allows each body to define the penalties for non-obedience to those rules.

There is an interesting factor here that is never mentioned, and that is the requirement in the Senate to have 61 votes to pass legislation. The word majority as included in the paragraph means 1 more than half. For example: in today's Senate the majority is 100/2=50 and one more, which should be the Vice-President's vote, for 51. There is no lawful requirement that allows 61. This rule was established to control the power in the Senate. The 61 vote requirement is clearly unconstitutional. Sometimes the Senate talks of the "Nuclear Option" which really means that they are going to revert to the Constitution's requirement of a majority to pass legislation. Wouldn't it more correct if the Senate would always follow the direction of the Constitution?

Article I, Section 5, Paragraph 2

> **Each House may determine the Rules of its Proceedings, punish its Members for disorderly Behavior, and, with the Concurrence of two thirds, expel a Member.**

This paragraph provides additional rules that the House of Representatives and the Senate can use to control its members and the rules to expel a member from the body.

Article I, Section 5, Paragraph 3

> **Each House shall keep a Journal of its Proceedings, and from time to time publish the same, excepting such Parts as may in their Judgment require Secrecy; and the Yeas and Nays of the Members of either House on any question shall, at the Desire of one fifth of those Present, be entered on the Journal.**

Here are additional details on how the Houses conduct their business. One of the requirements is for each House to have a journal of all activities and that the journal will be published. We are allowed access to this journal, which is called the

Congressional Record. The votes of each member will be recorded when one fifth of those present request it. The term "roll call" means that a check is being made to determine if there is a quorum present. The presence of each member is recorded in the Congressional Record when there is a roll call and a request is made that the results of the role call be recorded.

Article I, Section 5, Paragraph 4

Neither House, during the Session of Congress, shall, without the Consent of the other, adjourn for more than three days, nor to any other Place than that in which the two Houses shall be sitting.

This paragraph defines the rules for adjournment stating that neither body of Congress can adjourn independent of the other. This requirement keeps both Houses in session so that business can be completed. There is also a requirement that all business must be conducted in the official place where the Houses normally conduct business.

Article I, Section 6, Paragraph 1

Section 6. The Senators and Representatives shall receive a Compensation for their Services, to be ascertained by Law and paid out of the Treasury of the United States. They shall in all Cases, except

Treason, Felony, and Breach of the Peace, be privileged from Arrest during their Attendance at the Session of their respective Houses, and in going to and returning from the same; and for any Speech or Debate in either House, they shall not be questioned in any other Place.

Here are some detailed stipulations on how members of Congress are to be treated while in session.

- First, they are to receive a compensation from the federal government for their services.
- Second, they shall not be arrested while in session except for Treason, Felony, and Breach of the Peace.

What is Treason? The word treason appears seven times in the Constitution. Each time it is mentioned I will refer back to this paragraph. Here is the definition found in *Webster's Dictionary of 1828:*

"In the United States, treason is confined to the actual levying of war against the United States, or in adhering to their enemies, giving them aid and comfort.

Other countries have different definitions, but we are in the United States and that is the definition of treason during the period when the Constitution was written. The problem is the definition of war against the United States. We speak of the war on drugs, but is that really a war? Usually, a war is meant by one country's army shooting against another country's army. Today, often we are incorrectly using the word treason as a complaint against an individual that is attempting to change our culture and our way of life.

Webster's Dictionary of 1828 defines felony as:

"In common law, any crime which incurs the forfeiture of lands or goods.

This would be the definition for felony in the days of the Founding Fathers, and therefore the members of Congress can be arrested for this kind of crime.

What is a breach of the peace? That could also be called inciting to a riot. In today's world we have members of Congress, by their words and actions, inciting citizens to riot. That is a clear breach of the peace. It is time that some action was taken to curtail these activities.

- Third, they cannot be questioned for any speech or debate in any other place than in the House of Representatives or the Senate.

Today's media is constantly questioning, on radio and TV, the speeches and comments of the members of Congress. These are unconstitutional actions by the media. The problem is that the members of Congress want these questions and comments to be discussed by the media for political gain for themselves while causing political loss for any opponent.

Article I, Section 6, Paragraph 2

No Senator or Representative shall, during the Time for which he was elected, be appointed to any civil Office under the Authority of the United States which shall have been created, or the Emoluments whereof shall have been encreased, during such time; and no Person holding any Office under the United States shall be a Member of either House during his Continuance in Office.

What is an Emolument? From *Webster's Dictionary of 1828*:

"1. The profit arising from office or employment; that which is received as a

47

compensation for services, or which is annexed to the possession of office, as salary, feels and perquisites. or

" 2. Profit; advantage; gains in general.

In other words a member of Congress cannot have an increase in income resulting from their position in government, or income from a civilian job because of their position, or income from a civilian job created by the federal government.

Then it goes on to say that no person can have another federal government position while serving in Congress.

Article I, Section 7, Paragraph 1

Section 7. All bills for raising Revenue shall originate in the House of Representatives; but the Senate may propose or concur with Amendments as on other Bills.

This is a very important paragraph as it involves taxes and the people must have their representatives directly involved in taxation. No bill involving taxes or other revenue producing activities can originate in the Senate. The Senate can add amendments to such a bill, but it cannot start one.

Article I, Section 7, Paragraph 2

Every Bill which shall have passed the House of Representatives and the Senate shall, before it becomes a Law, be presented to the President of the United States. If he approve he shall sign it, but if not he shall return it, with his Objections, to that House in which it shall have originated, who shall enter the Objections at large on their Journal and proceed to reconsider it. If after such Reconsideration two thirds of that House shall agree to pass the Bill, it shall be sent, together with the Objections, to the other House, by which it shall likewise be reconsidered, and if approved by two thirds of that House, it shall become a Law. But in all such Cases the Votes of both Houses shall be determined by yeas and Nays, and the Names of the Persons voting for and against the Bill shall be entered on the Journal of each House respectively. If any Bill shall not be returned by the President within ten Days (Sundays excepted) after it shall have been presented to him, the Same shall be a Law, in like Manner as if he had signed it, unless the Congress by their Adjournment prevent its Return, in which Case it shall not be a Law.

These are the details of how a bill becomes a law. Several conditions are presented concerning vetoes. An interesting part concerns the last sentence. This is commonly called a pocket veto. When the President receives a bill he doesn't want to sign for some reason, and he knows that Congress will adjourn within the 10 day period he just puts it in a drawer and ignores it. After Congress adjourns it is automatically vetoed without his taking any action.

Article I, Section 7, Paragraph 3

> **Every Order, Resolution, or Vote to which the Concurrence of the Senate and House of Representatives may be necessary (except on a question of Adjournment) shall be presented to the President of the United States; and, before the Same shall take Effect, shall be approved by him, or, being disapproved by him, shall be repassed by two thirds of the Senate and House of Representatives, according to the Rules and Limitations prescribed in the Case of a Bill.**

This paragraph ensures that all actions of the Congress must be approved by the President following the rules established in paragraph 2 of this section.

Article I, Section 8, Paragraph 1

> **Section 8. The Congress shall have Power To lay and collect Taxes, Duties, Imposts and Excises, to pay the Debts and provide for the common Defense and general Welfare of the United States; but all Duties, Imposts, and Excises shall be uniform throughout the United States;**

Section 8 is one of the most important sections of the Constitution. This section outlines what the Congress can actually do. If it is not included in these 18 paragraphs, Congress is not allowed to do it!

Congress has chosen to totally ignore this section. They all know what it says, but do not pay any attention at all. Almost all activities of today's Congress are in violation of this section. There are so many violations that it would be almost impossible to list them all.

The first paragraph allows Congress to impose taxes on: "Duties, Imposts and Excises." These terms represent what we now call tariffs. The government originally financed a lot of its operations on these tariffs.

This paragraph then goes on to describe how they are to be used. The words "general Welfare of the United States" have been changed to anything that they want to spend on any one person or any group of people including foreign nations. General welfare of the United States does NOT include foreign countries! So all foreign aid is unconstitutional. Our taxes are not to be spent on European nations or any other nation! We are not responsible for the lives of the citizens of other countries. If individuals or private organizations want to do this that would be fine and good, but the United States government is prohibited from doing it by this paragraph.

The federal government is likewise prohibited from spending our tax dollars on any one United States citizen or business or group of citizens or businesses. Don't overlook that removing tax requirements with subsidies is the same as providing tax dollars. Subsidies of any kind to any person or business, no matter how well intentioned, is prohibited.

Article I, Section 8, Paragraph 2

To borrow money on the credit of the United States;

Congress is allowed to borrow money to fund the government, if desired and legally needed. But borrowing money means receiving the funds. When we borrow from a bank we get the money from the bank. When the government borrows money it must not borrow counterfeit money. All money borrowed from the current Federal Reserve or Central bank is counterfeit, similar to Monopoly money, as that organization has no actual money available. Therefore, since it is counterfeit money we have no legal requirement to pay the interest or the principle.

Article I, Section 8, Paragraph 3

To regulate Commerce with foreign Nations, and among the several States, and with the Indian tribes;

The first issue here is the word regulate. Regulate doesn't mean control. In the second part of the definition of the word regulate *Webster's Dictionary of 1828* states:

"2. To put in good order; as, to *regulate* the disordered state of a nation or its finances.

Since the Commerce of the United States was never disorderly there was no need for the supreme court to fiddle with it at all. But, Congress and the supreme court banded together to change this paragraph to mean whatever they wanted it to mean. In Volume 4 of my series *Liberty: Will it Survive the 21st Century?* I devoted 13 pages to this Commerce clause.

The federal government has expanded these sixteen words from what was originally intended, to laws and regulations that tell us what we can grow in our own gardens on our own property for our own use.

The misuse of this paragraph has destroyed our liberties on how we can use our own private property. We are abused as if we lived in a dictatorship. If all of the regulations and laws that have been written on the subject of commerce were enforced, we would have legions of government officials inspecting our property, our homes and our way of life.

Article I, Section 8, Paragraph 4

To establish an uniform Rule of Naturalization, and uniform Laws on the subject of Bankruptcies throughout the United States;

The uniform rules on naturalization were established and successfully used for many decades. But today much of that has been ignored because there are those in both of the political parties who would like a One World Order and that means abolishing country borders. That is why the Congress will not address the immigration laws and why so much illegal immigration is going on. As a people we have lost the desire to follow the Constitution, as it seems to get in our way. We must reestablish our immigration and naturalization laws and procedures so that the laws reflect what is best for our country as required in this paragraph of the Constitution.

The bankruptcy portion of the paragraph seems to be functioning. Finally, here is an item of this section the Congress and the federal government are actually following.

Article I, Section 8, Paragraph 5

To coin Money, regulate the Value thereof, and of foreign Coin, and fix the Standard of Weights and Measures;

This paragraph was first violated in 1791, only three years after the Constitution was ratified. The Founders did not authorize the Congress to hand over, to a private corporation, the power to create our money and control its value. In essence, Congress gave a private corporation the ability to control our entire nation's financial well being. There are forces in the world that control our lives through these central banks.

The first step in this control, in our country, occurred with the authorization of the First Bank of the United States, which was authorized in 1791 with a 20 year charter and was a central bank owned and controlled ultimately by the Bank of England. This bank was the first of three central banks in our country. The second one, the Second Bank of the United States, was authorized in 1816 with a 20 year charter and the third, the Federal Reserve, was authorized in 1913 with no ending date.

None of these are really banks as we know them. Central banks do not have any cash or money in their vaults. When these banks loan to governments, which is one of their main functions, they create or counterfeit the money at the time of the loan. Then they require repayment and interest on these loans even though no money was ever actually loaned. American citizens are actually required to pay interest on a non-debt debt. That simply means no money was loaned so there is no debt.

Central banks are not federal institutions. They are private institutions owned by the wealthiest individuals in the world. The profits of these central banks are then used to control the governments of the various countries through controlling the politicians with bribes and payoffs of one sort or another. This operation is covered in detail in volume 6 of my series *Liberty: Will it Survive the 21ˢᵗ Century?*

Next these central banks also control the value of the currency in the countries where they are established. This is done through the manipulation of the money supply. When they want a recession or a depreciation they use the banking system to destroy money. When they want inflation they use this same banking system to create money. This is the major cause of the business cycles that we are familiar with. They make profits during every business cycle as these cycles bankrupt individuals and businesses.

The whole banking process we are saddled with, is in complete violation of this paragraph of Section 8. The Constitution requires the Congress to coin the money and regulate the value of it. Many people have been taught that the term regulate had a different definition in colonial times. That is not true. The definition of regulate has not changed from then until now.

If the Congress coined, printed and issued the money of our nation there would be no debt. If the Congress truly regulated the value of the money, the business cycles would be of less importance. History shows us that there were recessions and depressions before the Federal Reserve and have been numerous recessions and depressions since the Federal Reserve was established. They have always been caused by the banking industry of the time and in every case these cycles make profits for those banks. The book *The Coming Battle* published in 1898 discusses in great detail how this was done during the last third of the 1800s..

Congress did establish the standards of weights and measures and still does. So this is another item that follows the Constitution.

Article I, Section 8, Paragraph 6

To provide for the Punishment of counterfeiting the Securities and current Coin of the United States;

The punishment for counterfeiting our money is provided for. The question is why is the largest counterfeiter of our money never prosecuted? This question refers to the Federal Reserve discussed in the above paragraph.

Article I, Section 8, Paragraph 7

To establish Post Offices and post Roads;

The post offices have been established and they are doing a moderate job. It's a pity that we see private mail systems doing it better and less expensively.

What are Post Roads? In Wikipedia we read that A **post road** is a **road** designated for the transportation of postal mail. In past centuries, only major towns had a **post** house and the **roads** used by

post riders or mail coaches to carry mail among them were particularly important ones or, due to the special attention given them, became so. RFD routes or Rural Free Delivery routes would be a form of Post Roads.

Article I, Section 8, Paragraph 8

> **To promote the Progress of Science and useful Arts by securing for limited Times to Authors and Inventors the exclusive Right to their respective Writings and Discoveries;**

This paragraph is another example of an area that the government actually follows with laws concerning patents, trademarks, and copyrights.

Article I, Section 8, Paragraph 9

> **To constitute Tribunals inferior to the supreme Court;**

Federal courts have been established that are inferior to the supreme court. All of these federal courts far exceed their authority as listed in Article III.

Article I, Section 8, Paragraph 10

To define and punish Piracies and Felonies committed on the high Seas, and Offenses against the Law of Nations;

In his *Commentaries on the Constitution of the United States* (1833) Book 3, Chapter 20, Joseph L. Story discussed the Power to Punish Piracies and Felonies on the High Seas as follows:

"This paragraph gave Congress sole and exclusive power "of appointing courts for the trial of piracies and felonies committed on the high seas." But there was no power expressly given to define and punish piracies and felonies. Congress, however, proceeded to pass an ordinance for the erection of a court for such trials, and prescribed the punishment of death upon conviction of the offense. But they never undertook to define, what piracies or felonies were. It was taken for granted, that these were sufficiently known and understood.

Then offenses against the Law of Nations is defined by Jon Roland of the Constitution Society in 1998:

"Offenses against the Law of Nations - It is important to understand what is and is not included in the phrase "Law of Nations." It means the underlying principles of right and justice among nations, and during the founding era the "Law of Nations" was not considered the same as the body of treaties and conventions between nations. The distinction goes back to ancient Roman Law.

"Briefly, the Law of Nations at the point of ratification in 1788 included the following general elements, taken from *Blackstone's Commentaries*, and prosecution of those who might violate them:

"(1) No attacks on foreign nations, their citizens, or shipping, without either a declaration of war or letters of marque and reprisal.

"(2) Honoring of the flag of truce, peace treaties, and boundary treaties. No entry across national borders without permission of national authorities.

"(3) Protection of wrecked ships, their passengers and crew, and their cargo, from depredation by those who might find them.

"(4) Prosecution of piracy by whomever might be able to capture the pirates, even if those making the capture or their nations had not been victims.

"(5) Care and decent treatment of prisoners of war.

"(6) Protection of foreign embassies, ambassadors, and diplomats, and of foreign ships and their passengers, crew, and cargo while in domestic waters or in port.

"(7) Honoring of extradition treaties for criminals who committed crimes in a nation with whom one has such a treaty who escapes to one's territory or are found on the high seas.

"And, although it was not yet firmly established with all nations in 1788,

"(8) Prohibition of enslavement of foreign nationals and international trading in slaves.

Article I, Section 8, Paragraph 11

To declare War, grant Letters of Marque and Reprisal, and make Rules concerning Captures on Land and Water;

It is clear in this paragraph that wars must be declared by Congress. The fact of the matter is that no war has been officially declared since World War II. The wars of today are wars of the United Nations, and we just send troops where the United Nations dictates. Consider all of the wars we have been involved in during this century alone.

On September 19, 2017 Senator Rand Paul pointed out that:

"What we have today is basically unlimited war — war anywhere, anytime, any place on the globe. I don't think anyone with an ounce of intellectual honesty believes these authorizations allow current wars we fight in seven countries."

We have completely lost the idea that Congress controls when we go to war, not the United Nations.

What was a letter of Marque? From Wikipedia we read:

"A letter of marque and reprisal was a government license in the Age of Sail that authorized a private person, known as a privateer or corsair, to attack and capture vessels of a nation at war with the issuer. Once captured, the privateer could then bring the case of that prize before their own admiralty court for condemnation and transfer of ownership to the privateer. A letter of marque and reprisal would include permission to cross an international border to effect a reprisal (take some action against an attack or injury) and was authorized by an issuing jurisdiction to conduct reprisal operations outside its borders.

"Popular among Europeans from the late Middle Ages up to the 19th century, cruising for enemy prizes with a letter of marque was considered an honorable calling that combined patriotism and profit. Such privateering contrasted with attacks and captures of random ships, which was unlicensed and known as piracy; piracy was almost universally reviled. In reality, the differences between privateers and pirates were often at best subtle, and at worst more a matter of interpretation.

Article I, Section 8, Paragraph 12

To raise and support Armies, but no Appropriation of Money to that Use shall be for a longer Term than two Years;

This is the only reference allowing an army and this reference only allows that army to exist for two years without additional authorization and appropriations.

Article I, Section 8, Paragraph 13

To provide and maintain a Navy;

It is interesting to note that the only military force permanently authorized by the Constitution is the Navy and by extension the Marines as they are the fighting force of the Navy.

Article I, Section 8, Paragraph 14

To make Rules for the Government and Regulation of the land and naval Forces;

Here is the requirement to ensure that the Navy is properly organized and regulated. The Congress was authorized to make rules for military forces when they were authorized.

Article I, Section 8, Paragraph 15

To provide for calling forth the Militia to execute the Laws of the Union, suppress Insurrections, and repel Invasions;

What is a militia?

"The militia of a country are the able bodied men organized into companies, regiments and brigades, with officers of all grades, and required by law to attend military exercises on certain days only, but at other times left to pursue their usual occupations." From *Webster's Dictionary of 1828.*

These are the citizens of the country with their own weapons. This is not a standing army, but would satisfy the need for a military force which is actually required in today's world. There is no authorization for a national standing army lasting more than two years.

Article I, Section 8, Paragraph 16

To provide for organizing, arming, and disciplining the Militia, and for governing such Part of them as may be employed in the Service of the United States, reserving to the States respectively the Appointment of the Officers and the Authority

of training the Militia according to the discipline prescribed by Congress;

In this paragraph we discover that the federal government is responsible for organizing the militia and providing the weapons and ammunition for each citizen. Then the States appoint the officers and conduct training as described by Congress. This function has been completely ignored throughout the entire history of the United States.

Today, instead of arming the citizens, the goal is to take away even the arms that the citizens buy for themselves. The whole concept of this Constitution has been turned completely upside down because no one is taught anything about it. In fact, most schools that claim to teach the Constitution really just teach the history and never the actual document itself. Even so called Constitutional scholars don't learn the Constitution. Instead, they learn the precedents established by the supreme court.

Article I, Section 8, Paragraph 17

To exercise exclusive Legislation in all Cases whatsoever, over such District (not exceeding ten Miles square) as may, by Cession of particular States and the Acceptance of Congress, become the Seat of the Government of the United States, and to exercise like Authority over all Places

purchased by the Consent of the Legislature of the State in which the Same shall be, for the Erection of Forts, Magazines, Arsenals, dock-Yards, and other needful Buildings;

This paragraph has been broadened to include any land that the federal government wants. Today all the government has to do to take any non-private land is to make an announcement and presto it's theirs. That's not exactly what the paragraph says, is it?

Except for the seat of government, or Washington, D.C. the steps listed here are as follows.

- First, the government decides what land it desires.
- Second, the government gets permission from the Legislature of the State involved.
- Third, if that request is approved, a price must be set and the land purchased in accordance with the rules that the State sets in its approval document.
- Fourth, the only purposes that the land can be used for is "the Erection of Forts, Magazines, Arsenals, dock-Yards, and other needful Buildings;" Needful buildings are the buildings required to maintain the forts, magazines, arsenals, and dock-yards.

There is no provision for national parks, national monuments, national forests, fish and game preserves etc. These are not now nor ever have been authorized for the federal government. All of these purposes are reserved for the States. I have covered this in great detail in Volumes 1, 3, and 6 of my series *Liberty: Will it Survive the 21ˢᵗ Century?*

Article I, Section 8, Paragraph 18

> **To make all Laws which shall be necessary and proper for carrying into Execution the foregoing Powers, and all other Powers vested by this Constitution in the Government of the United States, or in any Department or Officer thereof.**

Here is a very misunderstood paragraph. Some have defined it to mean that Congress can designate any organization or group to perform any task they want them to do. If this was actually the case, there would be no need for this section at all. Obviously this section was very important to the Founding Fathers. It limited the powers of the federal government that they were creating, and they knew that the new government would have to be limited. This paragraph is intended to allow Congress to establish other government agencies to help put the laws they authorized into effect.

Thus the treasury department was established to assist in coining and printing the money they would authorize. As an example, this paragraph does not give Congress the right to allow a privately owned company to create the money of the United States and then charge interest on the money they created for their own profit. The Federal Reserve is a complete abrogation of Congress' power and gives away it's lawfully authorized printing and coining of money responsibility.

Now that you have reviewed all of the paragraphs of Section 8, let's look at a relatively recent act of Congress. Remember when the government decreed that no incandescent light bulbs could be manufactured? This is a characteristic of a fascist government. Our nation is not fascistic. We are a Republic and as shown in this Section of Article I Congress has no power to enact this law. Congress took over a private industry and dictated what it could or could not manufacture. A characteristic of fascism is a political movement that takes over and controls corporations. This type of government existed in Italy from 1922 to 1943 under the dictatorship of Benito Mussolini.

Article I, Section 9, Paragraph 1

> **Section 9.** The Migration or Importation of such Persons as any of the States now existing shall think proper to admit, shall not be prohibited by the Congress prior to the year one thousand eight hundred and eight, but a Tax or duty may be imposed on such Importation, not exceeding ten dollars for each Person.

This section is devoted to items that Congress cannot do. It makes sure that these items are spelled out exactly so there won't be any misinterpretation.

This first paragraph is the key paragraph about slavery. Even though it doesn't say slavery it says "The migration or importation of such persons as any of the states now existing shall think proper to admit shall not be prohibited by the Congress." Who did the States import? Slaves and this paragraph requires that the importation of these slaves is prohibited after 1808.

This date, 1808, was the compromise that allowed the Southern States enough time to retire the debts on their plantations that were collateralized by the slaves. This was a pivotal paragraph, which the Southern States demanded or they wouldn't ratify the Constitution. Without this paragraph there would have been no United States of America because there would have been no Constitution. Then the Southern States did not keep this commitment and slavery continued until the Civil War. Problems that had their foundation in slavery still exist today. Perhaps, if the Southern States had kept this agreement many of the problems of the black race would never have arisen.

Article I, Section 9, Paragraph 2

The Privilege of the Writ of Habeas Corpus shall not be suspended, unless when in Cases of Rebellion or Invasion the public Safety may require it.

What is the "Privilege of the Writ of Habeas Corpus"? The Writ of Habeas Corpus is used to bring a prisoner or other detainee, often an institutionalized mental patient, before the court to determine if the person's imprisonment or detention is lawful. A habeas petition proceeds as a civil action against a state agent, usually a warden, who holds the defendant in custody. It is currently used to prevent unlawful imprisonment. The exception to the Writ of Habeas Corpus is during a temporary emergency affecting public safety.

Article I, Section 9, Paragraph 3

No Bill of Attainder or ex post facto Law shall be passed.

What is a Bill of Attainder? A Bill of Attainder is a legislative act that singles out an individual or group for punishment without a trial.

This was added to the Constitution because the English used this type of law to confiscate property. If a person were sentenced to death, their property was confiscated by the Crown. The Founders did not want this type of law on the books of the United States of America.

Ex post facto laws are laws that make illegal an act that was legal when the crime was committed. They also increase the penalties for an infraction after it has been committed and change the rules of evidence to make conviction easier.

This was a problem in the Revolutionary period. This is from Georgetown University:

Georgetown University Law Center
Ex Post Facto in the Civil Context: *Unbridled Punishment* by Jane H. Aiken, 1992

"The history of the Ex Post Facto Clause reveals the sharp departure that the United States Supreme Court has taken from what was originally intended when the Clause was included in the Constitution. Early debates focused on the invidious nature of all laws that had retrospective application.

"In addition, justices have not universally agreed that the term "ex post facto" reaches only retrospective criminal laws. For example, Justice Johnson in Satterlee v Matthewson strongly objected to the Court's holding in Calder v Bull, (1798) that the Ex Post Facto Clause applied only to criminal laws. Furthermore, some scholars have argued that former Chief Justice John Marshall opposed the Court's holding in Calder.

"The framers were clear on the harm to be avoided, and this harm can take both criminal and civil form. Having witnessed as colonists the potential for oppressiveness in government, the framers considered protection against ex post facto and other unjust laws essential for the new constitutional government.

Article I, Section 9, Paragraph 4

No Capitation or other direct, Tax shall be laid, unless in Proportion to the Census or Enumeration herein before directed to be taken.

Here is another paragraph that addresses taxes. The Founders knew that government always abuses tax laws and therefore included rules and prohibitions in several places. This paragraph directly addresses direct taxes and how they are to be used. Refer back to Article I, Section 2, paragraph 2, where direct taxes were specifically placed on the States. In this paragraph, these taxes had to be apportioned on the States based on their population, and the population was to be determined by a census. This concept is very important as it levys the taxes equally throughout the country.

This was one of the paragraphs that made direct taxes on the people so difficult. In the Sixteenth Amendment of 1913, the amendment had to say that this paragraph was to be ignored. Then the supreme court in 1916 upheld this alteration of the Constitution as constitutional. That means that the court found that statements right in the Constitution were unconstitutional. What a farce.

Article I, Section 9, Paragraph 5

No Tax or Duty shall be laid on Articles exported from any State.

This paragraph ensured that the States could not have tariffs on goods between the States so that goods could move freely throughout the nation.

Article I, Section 9, Paragraph 6

No Preference shall be given by any Regulation of Commerce or Revenue to the Ports of one State over those of another; nor shall Vessels bound to, or from, one State, be obliged to enter, clear, or pay Duties in another.

These items were included in the Constitution because, under the Articles of Confederation, States were levying duties on goods that were not even being shipped to them. Port taxes or duties were a problem that caused severe difficulties between the States. Also the commerce of all States had to be treated the same without preference.

We don't realize today the problems that occurred on shipments through and between the States. Remember prior to the Constitution every State was a separate government and had power and authority over its geographical area. The organization and government that the Constitution was establishing was taking power from the States and giving it to this federal government.

Article I, Section 9, Paragraph 7

> **No Money shall be drawn from the Treasury but in Consequence of Appropriations made by Law; and a regular Statement and Account of the Receipts and Expenditures of all public Money shall be published from time to time.**

This is called the Appropriations Clause and it is considered the cornerstone of Congress's "power of the purse." This is the excuse that has been used to allow Congress to spend money on anything it wants to. Article I, Section 8, was too limiting so the interpretation of this paragraph occurred to justify all of the unconstitutional expenditures.

Look at the actual wording and the phrase "Appropriations made by Law." That means expenditures which follow the law. The law is in Article I, Section 8. All spending must be authorized by that section. Anything that is spent that is not included in that section is unconstitutional.

This clause has been used to pervert the Constitution and to allow Congress to spend money on whatever or wherever it wants to spend it.

Article I, Section 9, Paragraph 8

> **No Title of Nobility shall be granted by the United States; and no Person holding any Office of Profit or Trust under them shall, without the Consent of the Congress, accept of any present, Emolument, Office, or Title, of any kind whatever, from any King, Prince, or foreign State.**

The Founders did not want any royalty in the new country so they included this paragraph. In addition, they did not want any government official to receive any gift from a foreign country that would influence them in any way.

It is interesting to note that Hillary Clinton violated this paragraph constantly using the Clinton Foundation and accepting payments from foreign countries, while Secretary of State. No one has ever pointed this out. But, that is probably because the federal government is staffed by many individuals that also violate this rule and who don't really care about the people, or the laws, or the Constitution.

Article I, Section 10, Paragraph 1

> **Section 10. No State shall enter into any Treaty, Alliance, or Confederation; grant Letters of Marque and Reprisal; coin Money; emit bills of Credit; make any Thing but gold and silver Coin a Tender in**

Payment of Debts; pass any Bill of Attainder, ex post facto Law, or Law impairing the Obligation of Contracts; or grant any Title of Nobility.

This section is a list of things the States cannot do. It begins with a list of the items that have been reserved to the federal government. Since this paragraph actually allows the States to use gold and silver as a tender of payment some States have recently taken advantage of this by passing laws that allow gold and silver to be used as a medium of exchange.

Article I, Section 10, Paragraph 2

No State shall, without the Consent of the Congress, lay any Imposts or Duties on Imports or Exports, except what may be absolutely necessary for executing its inspection laws; and the net Produce of all Duties and Imposts, laid by any State on Imports or Exports, shall be for the Use of the Treasury of the United States; and all such Laws shall be subject to the Revision and Control of the Congress.

Here is a firm control on the States preventing them from using import fees. But, when absolutely necessary the States can charge fees for inspecting imports, but any fees paid on imports that exceed expenses will be forwarded to the United States

Treasury. Even those laws for inspections must be approved by Congress.

Article I, Section 10, Paragraph 3

No State shall, without the Consent of Congress, lay any Duty of Tonnage; keep Troops or Ships of War in time of Peace; enter into any Agreement or Compact with another State, or with a foreign Power; or engage in War, unless actually invaded or in such imminent Danger as will not admit of delay.

This paragraph continues with items reserved to the federal government that States cannot do unless Congress gives consent.

The provision that the States cannot enter into any Agreement or Compact with another State, or with a foreign Power is quite important. States might have gone behind the federal government's back and made agreements with other nations that could have jeopardized the security of the nation as a whole. The prohibition for States to combine with other States is for the same national protection. Any agreements of this type would always be against the Constitution.

In today's political climate large groups of several thousand individuals have approached our borders demanding they be allowed to enter the United

States. This is an invasion. Based on the words, "engage in War, unless actually invaded" States are allowed to use state troops to protect their borders.

ARTICLE II

The Executive Branch

Article II, Section 1, Paragraph 1

Section 1. The executive Power shall be vested in a President of the United States of America. He shall hold his Office during the Term of four Years and, together with the Vice President, chosen for the same Term, be elected as follows.

In this paragraph the power of the executive is placed in the hands of a President elected for four years. It also states that the Vice-President is also elected for four years.

Article II, Section 1, Paragraph 2

Each State shall appoint, in such Manner as the Legislature thereof may direct, a Number of Electors equal to the whole Number of Senators and Representatives to which the State may be entitled in the Congress; but no Senator or Representative, or Person holding an Office of Trust or Profit under the United States, shall be appointed an Elector.

The first step is to select the Electoral College and each State was allowed to determine how that would be done. There are prohibitions listing some officials who may not be selected as an elector.

Article II, Section 1, Paragraph 3

The electors shall meet in their respective States and vote by Ballot for two Persons, of whom one at least shall not be an Inhabitant of the same State with themselves. And they shall make a List of all the Persons voted for, and of the Number of Votes for each; which List they shall sign and certify, and transmit sealed to the Seat of the Government of the United States, directed to the President of the Senate. The President of the Senate shall, in the Presence of the Senate and House of Representatives, open all the Certificates, and the Votes shall then be counted. The Person having the greatest Number of Votes shall be the President, if such Number be a Majority of the whole Number of Electors appointed; and if there be more than one who have such Majority, and have an equal Number of Votes, then the House of Representatives shall immediately chuse by Ballot one of them for President; and if no Person have a Majority, then from the five highest on the List the said House shall in like Manner chuse the President. But in choosing the President, the Votes shall be taken by States, the Representation from each State having one Vote; a quorum for this Purpose shall consist of a Member or Members from two thirds of the states, and a majority of all the States shall be necessary to a Choice. In every

Case, after the Choice of the President, the Person having the greatest Number of Votes of the Electors shall be the Vice President. But if there should remain two or more who have equal Votes, the Senate shall chuse from them by Ballot the Vice President.

The best way to explain the election process of the second and third paragraphs of Section 1 is to do it at one time. The changes deviating from the Constitution concerning the election of the President and the Vice-President were brought about in steps. The first step occurred in the election year of 1800, which was the first year of real political party control. In brief, political parties do not work. They foster evil and all kinds of horrible nonsense. President Washington spent nearly one third of his Farewell Address warning us of the evils of political parties. The second step in the process was the ratification of the Twelfth Amendment which created two separate lists, one for President and one for Vice-President.

The Founders established our country as a Republic NOT a Democracy. They reviewed governments that had been democracies and determined that that system did not work. A democracy is similar to two wolves and one sheep deciding what's for dinner. In a democracy the minority is always overruled by the majority. As you review our current political party system that factor is apparent over and over again.

The Electoral College was established to keep presidential elections free from becoming a popularity contest. They wanted the most qualified individual selected, not the one who could get the most people to vote for him. Look at what our presidential election has become. The elections of our country are a complete shambles. There is so much election fraud that now we can never really know who was actually elected. This has occurred because of the political party system and it is getting worse every year.

Section 1 paragraph 3 provides detailed procedures for electing the President. First, special individuals are selected by each State to serve as members of the Electoral College. The number of individuals is determined by the number of seats each State has in the Congress. This provides a proportionate number of delegates in relation to the population of each State. Each of these individuals nominates, the Constitution uses the word votes, two persons, one from their State and the other from a different State. These nominations would undoubtedly be the best individuals the Electoral College members could choose. There would be no politicking or pressure on who the Electoral Officials nominate.

The Electoral Officials of each State meet together, on the same date in every State, and each individual selects those two people he thinks would do the best job as President of the United States. These nominations are then tallied by each State and sent to the Senate of the United States under a seal. There, all of the nominations of every state are tallied. The individual receiving the most nominations would be president if that number was the majority of those submitted. If not, then a list of the five with the highest number of nominations is provided to the House of Representatives which then selects the President from those five individuals. Each State has one vote. The Vice President is the remaining presidential candidate with the most Electoral nominations after the President has been selected. No political party or politics is involved.

Isn't it obvious that this system would always select individuals of the highest caliber? It would never be a popularity contest or a contest of sound bites or a selection of who would pay the people the most from the federal treasury. It would be a selection of the best available. Think of all the lying and name calling that goes on in our current election process that would be eliminated. Real patriotic leaders who would follow the Constitution would be nominated.

A major part of destroying this inspired system was to change what the Electoral College did. That was accomplished with the Twelfth Amendment. The major change in that amendment was how the Electoral College performed its nominations. This changed the office that the nominations were for. Instead of two people for President now would nominate one person for President and one person for Vice-President. This created two pools for the Senate and the House of Representatives to review. The next step was to form two political parties to choose who would be considered for President and Vice-President and have the citizens select which of these individuals they wanted for President and Vice President. In actual fact the Electoral College was replaced by the political parties.

Then the Electoral College was given the task of ratifying what the popular vote decided. These steps were in place by the election year of 1800 even though the Twelfth Amendment wasn't ratified until June of 1804. The Twelfth Amendment was completely superfluous because the political parties were already in place.

The election year of 1800 was a fierce smear campaign with lies and falsehoods on every side trying to destroy the character of the other candidate. It was the beginnings of what we currently see in our political arena.

No amendment was ever proposed or ratified that changed the election process allowing the political parties to select the candidates bypassing the Electoral College completely. Our current election process is completely unconstitutional and has been ever since the election during the year of 1800.

On January 3, 2019 Democratic Congressman Steve Cohen from Tennessee, a senior member of the House Judiciary Committee, introduced a Constitutional Amendment to eliminate the Electoral College and provide for the direct election of the President and Vice President of the United States. If the uninformed people of the United States were to pass this amendment then none of the smaller states would ever again be a part of the election of the President. California and the larger Eastern states would completely dominate the elections for the President. Of course this is the goal of the Democratic Party because they know that they dominate these urban areas.

Article II, Section 1, Paragraph 4

The Congress may determine the Time of chusing the Electors and the Day on which they shall give their Votes, which Day shall be the same throughout the United States.

The Founders gave the responsibility for setting the day the electors met to select their nominations. The key was that every State would use the same day to make their nominations. And there is a firm requirement that these electors would actually meet within the States themselves.

Article II, Section 1, Paragraph 5

No person except a natural born Citizen, or a Citizen of the United States at the time of the Adoption of this Constitution, shall be eligible to the Office of President; neither shall any person be eligible to that Office who shall not have attained to the Age of thirty five Years and been fourteen Years a Resident within the United States.

Here are the qualifications for the President and also for the Vice President because he could one day be President. In the beginning the rules had to allow for the beginning of the Republic. Today everyone has to meet the natural born citizen requirement.

There is now some debate about who is a natural born citizen. Mostly this is from political parties or individuals who want to get around this requirement. If we were electing the President properly, there would be no problem.

The following is an opinion on the natural born requirement from the Legal Information Institute:

> "Anyone born after the adoption of the U.S. Constitution in 1787 must be a "natural born Citizen" of the United States to constitutionally fill the office of President or Vice-President. The constitution does not expressly define "natural born". Consensus exists that anyone born on U.S. soil and subject to its jurisdiction at birth is a natural born citizen, regardless of parental citizenship.

> "In 1790, the First Congress passed a naturalization act stating that "the children of citizens of the United States, that may be born beyond sea, or out of the limits of the United States, shall be considered as natural-born citizens. This act may indicate that the framers of the constitution (many of whom served in the First Congress) contemplated that such foreign-born citizens would be

considered natural born. It is felt that this thinking is also in line with the definition of natural born in English law at the time and thus that such citizens are "natural born" as used in the constitution.

Article II, Section 1, Paragraph 6

In Case of the Removal of the President from Office, or of his Death, Resignation, or Inability to discharge the Powers and Duties of the said Office, the Same shall devolve on the Vice President, and the Congress may by Law provide for the Case of Removal, Death, Resignation, or Inability, both of the President and Vice President, declaring what Officer shall then act as President; and such Officer shall act accordingly until the Disability be removed or a President shall be elected.

After reading this paragraph closely, many questions can arise, not the least of which is who shall decide that the President is not fit for duty and should be removed from office? The text of the Twenty-fifth Amendment purportedly answers the questions of this paragraph, but in actuality it does not. In volume three of *The Founders' Constitution*, the problems of this paragraph are not really discussed either. This paragraph of the Constitution is the poorest, least clear of the entire Constitution. That is illustrated by the unjust treatment that President Trump is being subjected to,

The Founders knew that instances could arise where the President could no longer function or where he could no longer be allowed to continue to serve. Therefore, provisions for removal were included. Then Congress was tasked with the responsibility for establishing who would be next in line, but with the party system we are currently plagued with, it is possible that the Congress could be completely corrupt. In that case they could remove the president and put another corrupt individual in his place. That corrupt individual would then exercise the power of the President.

Congress has addressed the succession of the presidency with Acts in 1792, 1886, and 1947. Then in 2002 the Secretary of Homeland Security was added to the list amid some controversy. The controversy was where to place the Secretary in the order. This was resolved in 2006. So far, there has never been a requirement for any other than the Vice-President to assume the office.

When there is a vacancy in offices of both President and Vice President; officers eligible to act are prescribed by (3 U.S.C. § 19, 1947):

"(a) (1) If, by reason of death, resignation, removal from office, inability, or failure to qualify, there is neither a President nor Vice President to discharge the powers and duties of the office of President, then the Speaker of the House of Representatives shall, upon his resignation as Speaker and as Representative in Congress, act as President.

"(2) The same rule shall apply in the case of the death, resignation, removal from office, or inability of an individual acting as President under this subsection.

"(b) If, at the time when under subsection (a) of this section a Speaker is to begin the discharge of the powers and duties of the office of President, there is no Speaker, or the Speaker fails to qualify as Acting President, then the President pro tempore of the Senate shall, upon his resignation as President pro tempore and as Senator, act as President.

"(c) An individual acting as President under subsection (a) or subsection (b) of this section shall continue to act until the expiration of the then current Presidential term, except that –

"(1) if his discharge of the powers and duties of the office is founded in whole or in part on the failure of both the President-elect and the Vice-President-elect to qualify, then he shall act only until a President or Vice President qualifies; and

"(2) if his discharge of the powers and duties of the office is founded in whole or in part on the inability of the President or Vice President, then he shall act only until the removal of the disability of one of such individuals.

"(d) (1) If, by reason of death, resignation, removal from office, inability, or failure to qualify, there is no President pro tempore to act as President under subsection (b) of this section, then the officer of the United States who is highest on the following list, and who is not under disability to discharge the powers and duties of the office of President shall act as President: Secretary of State, Secretary of the Treasury, Secretary of Defense, Attorney General, Secretary of the Interior, Secretary of Agriculture, Secretary of Commerce, Secretary of Labor, Secretary of Health and Human Services, Secretary of Housing and Urban Development, Secretary of

95

Transportation, Secretary of Energy, Secretary of Education, Secretary of Veterans Affairs, Secretary of Homeland Security.

"(2) An individual acting as President under this subsection shall continue so to do until the expiration of the then current Presidential term, but not after a qualified and prior-entitled individual is able to act, except that the removal of the disability of an individual higher on the list contained in paragraph (1) of this subsection or the ability to qualify on the part of an individual higher on such list shall not terminate his service.

"(3) The taking of the oath of office by an individual specified in the list in paragraph (1) of this subsection shall be held to constitute his resignation from the office by virtue of the holding of which he qualifies to act as President.

"(e) Subsections (a), (b), and (d) of this section shall apply only to such officers as are eligible to the office of President under the Constitution. Subsection (d) of this section shall apply only to officers appointed, by and with the advice and consent of the Senate, prior to the time of the death, resignation, removal from office, inability, or failure to qualify, of the President pro tempore, and only to officers not under impeachment by the House of Representatives at the time the powers and duties of the office of President devolve upon them.

"(f) During the period that any individual acts as President under this section, his compensation shall be at the rate then provided by law in the case of the President.

This succession has been modified several times with the addition of new cabinet positions. The creation of the Department of Homeland Security in 2002 caused controversy that delayed its secretary being placed in the succession order.

Many in the Congress felt the Secretary of Homeland Security should have been placed higher in the order – the rationale being that, as the officer responsible for disaster relief and security, the Secretary would be more capable of acting as President than, say, the Secretary of Housing and Urban Development. It was proposed that he be granted the position held by the Secretary of the Navy prior to the formation of the Department of Defense. In the 109th Congress, legislation was introduced to place the Secretary of Homeland Security into the line of succession after the Attorney General, but the bill expired at the end of the 109th Congress and was not reintroduced.

The matter remained unresolved until March 9, 2006, when the Act was amended to add the Secretary of Homeland Security after the Secretary of Veterans Affairs.

A total of 18 positions have been listed in order to fulfill the office of President.

Article II, Section 1, Paragraph 7

> **The President shall, at stated Times, receive for his Services a Compensation, which shall neither be increased nor diminished during the Period for which he shall have been elected; and he shall not receive within that Period any other Emolument from the United States, or any of them.**

The compensation for the President is authorized in this paragraph. The rule that no other compensation from the federal government or any of the States is also established.

In addition under a criminal conflict of interest statute, 18 U.S.C. § 209:

> "An executive branch employee is generally prohibited from receiving compensation from an outside source for doing his or her Government job. More specifically, unless an exception applies, an employee may not receive any salary or contribution to or supplementation of salary, from any source other than the Government, as compensation for services as a Government employee. Salary, or any contribution to or supplementation of salary, can be anything of monetary value received by the employee, including both lump-sum payments and periodic payments.

An emolument can be considered to be any gain from whatever source. This paragraph states that no emolument can be received by the president from the United States government or any State government during his term of office.

Article II, Section 1, Paragraph 8

Before he enter on the Execution of his Office, he shall take the following Oath or Affirmation: "I do solemnly swear (or affirm) that I will faithfully execute the Office of President of the United

99

States, and will, to the best of my Ability, preserve, protect, and defend the Constitution of the United States."

This paragraph establishes the oath of office and the words that are required. All officers of the government are required to take this oath. It is a pity that the oath is held in such low regard. Today government officials take this oath as required and then violate it prior to the end of the day it was administered.

January 3, 2019 Kyrsten Sinema a newly elected Congresswoman from Arizona would not put her hand on the Bible when being sworn in by Pence. She selected a book from the Library of Congress containing the texts of the U.S. and Arizona constitutions. There is no constitutional requirement that the Bible be used and many different books were used this year for incoming members of Congress. This just shows the departure and continual declining of our country away from Christianity. Several comments were made on social media that they were pleased to see people swearing to uphold our Constitution and our laws, and not some holy book. Historically, if someone would not swear or affirm their oath of office on the Bible, they were not to be sworn in because they could not be trusted.

Article II, Section 2, Paragraph 1

Section 2. The President shall be Commander in Chief of the Army and Navy of the United States, and of the Militia of the several States when called into the actual Service of the United States; he may require the Opinion, in writing, of the principal Officer in each of the executive Departments upon any Subject relating to the Duties of their respective Offices, and he shall have Power to grant Reprieves and Pardons for Offenses against the United States, except in Cases of Impeachment.

This paragraph establishes the President's power over the military. The Founders wanted the military to be under civilian authority based on the historical misuse of military power that took over the civil governments. This paragraph established the chain of command for the military.

It also gives the President the authority to ask for the opinions, on any subject, of each of the executive departments in the Executive Branch of the federal government.

The "and" preceded by the comma establishes an additional authority to grant Reprieves and Pardons. It is interesting to note that this power has often been abused when significant donations have been made to the election war-chest. It seems money often trumps discretion.

Recently, the discussion has covered the President's power to pardon himself. There is no prohibition in the Constitution as to who he can pardon, so it follows that maybe he can pardon himself. That idea has been discussed in today's vindictive treatment of President Trump. But, don't ask the supreme court for its opinion on this matter. They don't seem to have ever read the document and appear to have no idea what it actually means.

Article II, Section 2, Paragraph 2

> **He shall have Power, by and with the Advice and Consent of the Senate, to make Treaties, provided two thirds of the Senators present concur; and he shall nominate, and by and with the Advice and Consent of the Senate shall appoint, Ambassadors, other public Ministers and Consuls, Judges of the supreme Court, and all other Officers of the United States whose Appointments are not herein otherwise provided for, and which shall be established by Law; but the Congress may by Law vest the Appointment of such inferior Officers as they think proper in the President alone, in the Courts of Law, or in the Heads of Departments.**

This is a very important paragraph as it determines the power of the President with regard to treaties. It is very clear that the Senate must consent to any treaty. If the Senate doesn't review the treaty or there is no consent, there is no enforceable treaty.

Now refer to Article VI to see what force treaties have with regard to the laws of our country. Ever since 1796, the supreme court has consistently gotten it wrong.

This paragraph also establishes that the consent of the Senate is required to approve ambassadors, other public ministers and consuls, justices of the supreme court, and all other officers of the United States whose appointments are not herein otherwise provided for.

What does that phrase "not herein otherwise provided for" mean? "Herein" would refer to the Constitution itself, therefore "not herein otherwise provided for" would mean if the Constitution does not provide for an appointment of an official then consent of the Senate is required. Then the phrase "and which shall be established by law" gives the Congress the power to establish appointments that require the consent of the Senate. Note how President Obama violated this paragraph over and over by appointing Czars to government positions as quasi cabinet members. Just one of the multitude of constitutional violations of that President.

Then there is an additional power of the Congress. They can establish the appointments of inferior officers who will not require the consent of the Senate. Those Czars were not established as inferior government appointments by the Congress.

Article II, Section 2, Paragraph 3

> **The President shall have power to fill up all Vacancies that may happen during the Recess of the Senate, by granting Commissions which shall expire at the End of their next Session.**

Finally the president can fill vacancies without the consent of the Senate when it is not in session. But in those instances the appointment will expire at the end of the next session unless the Senate consents during that session.

Article II, Section 3, Paragraph 1

> **Section 3. He shall from time to time give to the Congress information of the State of the Union, and recommend to their Consideration such Measures as he shall judge necessary and expedient; he may, on extraordinary Occasions, convene both Houses, or either of them, and in Case of Disagreement between them with Respect to the Time of Adjournment, he may adjourn them**

to such Time as he shall think proper; he shall receive Ambassadors and other public Ministers; he shall take Care that the Laws be faithfully executed; and shall Commission all the Officers of the United States.

Here a few administrative details, requirements and additional responsibilities of the President are listed. The State of the Union report is specified along with the privilege of recommending such measures that he thinks necessary.

He can, when necessary, convene both Houses of Congress or either one of them and can settle disagreements on the date of adjournment even by determining the date he thinks is proper.

He is granted the authority to receive ambassadors and heads of State in the name of the United States of America. He is responsible for ensuring that the laws of the the United States are enforced properly.

Finally, he is required to commission all of the officers of the military services. In August of 1965 I was commissioned as an officer of the United States Air Force by Lyndon Baines Johnson and given the rank of a 2nd Lieutenant.

Article II, Section 4, Paragraph 1

Section 4. The President, Vice President, and all civil Officers of the United States, shall be removed from Office on Impeachment for, and Conviction of, Treason, Bribery, or other high Crimes and Misdemeanors.

What is treason? Refer to Article I, Section 6, Paragraph 1

A high crime refers to the position of the individual committing the crime and not the crime itself. A lie told by the CEO of a company is far worse than a lie uttered by the company custodian. The higher the position in an organization that a person occupies the greater the damage done by his dishonesty.

High crimes refers to those crimes committed by people in authority, and especially those who are charged with securing the public trust. It is one thing if a teenager of a church congregation commits the act of fornication. It is entirely more severe if the Pastor engages in the same activity.

ARTICLE III

The Judicial Branch

Article III, Section 1

> **Section 1. The judicial Power of the United States shall be vested in one supreme Court, and in such inferior Courts as the Congress may from time to time ordain and establish. The Judges, both of the supreme and inferior Courts, shall hold their Offices during good Behavior, and shall, at stated Times, receive for their Services a Compensation, which shall not be diminished during their Continuance in Office.**

This is the Article that has resulted in many of the worst violations of the Constitution. These violations have set the stage for the removal of most of our freedoms. I devoted 1/3 of volume 4 in my series *Liberty: Will it Survive the 21st Century?* covering just a few of the worst violations of the supreme court. The violations are so severe that they exceed anything that might be considered reasonable.

The problem began in earnest in 1803, when John J. Marshall was Chief Justice. The case on which the entire foundation of these violations rests is Marbury v Madison, and this case is cited continually as the basis of all the illegal decisions. Marshall had the gall to state in his decision of this case that any law that violated the Constitution was null and void. That is correct, but then he went on to say that the supreme court had the responsibility to make that decision. Later Thomas Jefferson responded that the decision of the constitutionally of a law rested with the people. He said that members of the court would have normal bias and were not capable of making these decisions for the entire country.

The result of this decision in Marbury v Madison was that the supreme court has been changing the Constitution to make it say whatever they wanted it to say for the past 215 years and stripping us of most of our rights. In addition, another result of this decision is that the court is making laws with their decisions in violation of Article I, Section 1, Paragraph 1. This is the very first sentence of the Constitution and clearly states "All legislative Powers herein granted shall be vested in a Congress of the United States."

The term used to justify these appalling violations was **judicial review.**

Let's look at the the first section. Note the first three words in both Section 1 and Section 2 are "The judicial Power." This emphasis simply means that the power of the court is limited to the words following that phrase. In Section 1 the words are "of the United States shall be vested in one supreme Court, and in such inferior Courts as the Congress may from time to time ordain and establish." These words in this section specify who can use this power.

Here we have one supreme court and some inferior courts that Congress authorizes. These are all federal courts and as such must follow the federal Constitution. Notice the word supreme is not capitalized. The Constitution doesn't set the supreme court above any courts except the inferior courts of the federal government. This is not a hierarchy of courts of the United States. These are just two levels of courts of the federal government.

The section goes on to say they will hold their offices during good behavior. A review of the good behavior of the supreme court justices done by Mark Levin in his book *Men in Black* reveals that the behavior of many of these justices indicates that they should have been impeached. The section goes on to provide a compensation for their services which shall not be reduced during their continuance in office. There is no term indicated. The Constitution **doesn't** provide them a lifetime appointment, but the words of this section have been interpreted that way.

Article III, Section 2, Paragraph 1

> **Section 2. The judicial Power shall extend to all Cases, in Law and Equity, arising under this Constitution, the Laws of the United States, and Treaties made, or which shall be made, under their Authority; - to all Cases affecting Ambassadors, other public Ministers and Consuls; - to all Cases of admiralty and maritime Jurisdiction; - to Controversies to which the United States shall be a Party; - to Controversies between two or more States; - between a State and Citizens of another State; - between Citizens of different States; - between Citizens of the same State claiming Lands under Grants of different States; and between a State, or the Citizens thereof, and foreign States, Citizens, or Subjects.**

This second use of the term judicial power states what this power can be used for or what is the jurisdiction or authority of the federal courts specified in Section 1.

As we read this paragraph let us break it down to understand it better. In the first part, we see:

- The judicial Power shall extend to all Cases,
- in Law and Equity, arising under (here are listed 2 major laws)
- this Constitution, (and)
- the Laws of the United States, (then it goes on to include treaties)
- and Treaties made, or which shall be made,
- under their Authority; (whose authority? the Constitution and the laws of the United States)

This first part of this paragraph establishes the authority that the justices of the federal courts must use when applying the judicial power to the cases brought before it. The authority is established as the Constitution and then the laws of the United States which are accordance with the Constitution. It states that treaties will be law only when they follow the Constitution and the laws of the United States.

Then, in the second part, eight and only eight types of cases, for the federal courts to review, are listed: Note when you look at the actual Constitution, in almost every case each type is set apart by a semicolon and a dash so they are easily identified.

- • - to all Cases affecting Ambassadors, other public Ministers, and Consuls;
- • - to all Cases of admiralty and maritime Jurisdiction;
- • - to Controversies to which the United States shall be a Party;
- • - to Controversies between two or more States;
- • - between a State and Citizens of another State;
- • - between Citizens of different States;
- • - between Citizens of the same State claiming Lands under Grants of different States;
- • - and between a State, or the Citizens thereof, and foreign States, Citizens, or Subjects.

Do you see any authority to review the constitutionality of any federal law passed by Congress? **No!** The federal courts are bound to these specific types of cases. There is also no authority to review any laws of the States nor their constitutions. These are federal courts and are limited to those items listed in the Constitution.

So when Marshall wrote in his decision on Marbury v Madison that any law in violation of the Constitution was null and void, he was correct. But he had no authority to decide that the supreme court could decide if the law was constitutional or not. His comments about judicial review are actually

112

unconstitutional and therefore null and void per his own admission. In summary, Article III of the Constitution grants only one power: to judge cases.

At this point we must get an understanding of the difference between case law and common law. Common law is God's law or Nature's law and doesn't change. Case law is precedent law or law that changes as different judges decide what to do, based on their own outlook at the time. This type of law changes and all lawyers and judges must keep up with the changes. This concept is often called the Living Constitution. The Constitution is a contract, and contracts don't change unless all parties agree in writing. It isn't a living document; it is the rule of law and the supreme law of the land as we will discover in Article VI.

The idea of the Living Constitution is based on precedent law. But there is an interesting effect of these precedent setting decisions that change the Constitution. As we know, there is an evil influence lurking in our mortal or natural condition. This influence has the tendency to change established customs and rules. These changes often result in a changing of our culture and the result is more often than not in a direction that is not wholesome or moral.

Now how does this tie in with precedents? Notice how when the supreme court makes a decision that does not follow this trend of society, there is almost an immediate new case on that issue or a very similar issue. That trend continues until the court makes a decision that follows the trend and then all of a sudden that decision becomes law and a new case seldom ever makes it to the supreme court again. The result is that when evil prevails it becomes a precedent, but good usually doesn't set a precedent. An example of that type of precedent setting could be that a fetus becomes nothing but a tissue which justifies abortion. Ponder that concept as you observe what happens in our court system.

Article III, Section 2, Paragraph 2

> **In all Cases affecting Ambassadors, other public Ministers, and Consuls, and those in which a State shall be Party, the supreme Court shall have original Jurisdiction. In all the other Cases before mentioned, the supreme Court shall have appellate Jurisdiction, both as to Law and Fact, with such Exceptions and under such Regulations as the Congress shall make.**

What does original jurisdiction mean? It simply means that the supreme court sees the case first, while appellate jurisdiction means the supreme court reviews cases of other courts. What other courts?

The inferior federal courts. In what cases does any federal court have original or appellate jurisdiction? Only those cases that they are listed in Section 2 paragraph 1 of this article. Those are the only cases within the federal court's judicial power.

What does the phrase "under such Regulations as the Congress shall make" mean? That is defining the responsibility of the Congress to keep the Judicial Branch under control. When the Judicial Branch exceeds its authority, which it has done repeatedly ever since 1803, it is the responsibility of Congress to stop it.

The Congress represents the people and is also supposed to represent the states, which are the two powers that created the Constitution in the first place. As our representatives they should look out for our interests whenever the Judicial Branch goes afield. Question: do you remember any instance when Congress has told the supreme or other federal courts that they have exceeded their judicial power? In the past few years there have been numerous highly visible instances when Congress had the responsibility to control the Judiciary Branch and it has failed to do so.

Article III, Section 2, Paragraph 3

> **The Trial of all Crimes, except in Cases of Impeachment, shall be by Jury; and such Trial shall be held in the State where the said Crimes shall have been committed; but when not committed within any State, the Trial shall be at such Place or Places as the Congress may by Law have directed.**

This paragraph applies to the country as a whole and not just to the federal courts. It contains the authority and instruction to try all crimes in the United States with juries. These crimes are to be tried in the State where the crimes were committed. Impeachment trials are exempted from this requirement as they will always be federal government actions and will be based on this Constitution.

If the crime was not committed in a State then the Congress can determine where the trials will be held.

Article III, Section 3, Paragraph 1

> **Section 3. Treason against the United States shall consist only in levying War against them or in adhering to their Enemies, giving them Aid and Comfort. No Person shall be convicted of Treason unless on the Testimony of two Witnesses to the same overt Act, or on Confession in open Court.**

What is treason?   Refer to Article I, Section 6, Paragraph 1

Treason is the only crime specifically defined in the Constitution, and according to this paragraph a person is guilty of treason only if he goes to war against the United States or there is a war against the United States.   Treason also applies if a person adheres to the enemy and gives the enemy "aid or comfort." What does adhering to the enemy mean? It means actions agreeing with the enemy or actions that give support to the enemy. There must be two or more witnesses providing testimony of the same overt act or the accused gives a confession in open court.

Article III, Section 3, Paragraph 2

The Congress shall have Power to declare the Punishment of Treason, but no Attainder of Treason shall work Corruption of Blood or Forfeiture except during the Life of the Person attainted.

What is treason?   Refer to Article I, Section 6, Paragraph 1

The first part states that Congress is the only power authorized to declare a punishment of treason.

This prevents any other court from trying anyone for treason.

The last part of this paragraph is very difficult for us in today's language. What does "no Attainder of Treason shall work Corruption of Blood" mean? It simply means that the guilty person is the only one who can be punished for the crime. His friends or family cannot be punished if they were not involved in the crime. The next part of the sentence means that the punishment can only be for the life of the convicted individual.

The total meaning of this phrase should also include any punishment for any crime not just for treason. That is not exactly specified in the Constitution but I would expect this paragraph to include all punishments.

Refer back to Section 2, Paragraph 1 of this Article. We cannot leave this subject until we have discussed admiralty and maritime jurisdiction. For a further discussion on this topic, review Appendix 1 at the end of the book.

ARTICLE IV

The States and the Federal Government

Article IV, Section 1

> **Section 1. Full Faith and Credit shall be given in each State to the public Acts, Records and judicial Proceedings of every other State. And the Congress may by general Laws prescribe the Manner in which such Acts, Records, and Proceedings shall be proved, and the Effect thereof.**

This Article covers miscellaneous items between States.   The intent is to keep peace between the States and solve problems before they arise.   The following is from the Annenberg Classroom which is an internet site teaching civics education.

"The first section ensures that states respect and honor the state laws and court orders of other states, even when their own laws are different. For example, if citizens of New Jersey marry, divorce, or adopt children in New Jersey, Florida must recognize these actions as valid even if the marriage or divorce would not have been possible under Florida law. Similarly, if a court in one state orders a person to pay

119

money or to stop a certain behavior, the courts in other states must recognize and enforce that state's order.

The next part is also from the Annenberg Classroom and explains that Congress has the power to control how records are recognized.

"This section also gives Congress the power to determine how states recognize records and laws from other states and how they enforce each others' court orders. For example, Congress may pass a federal law that specifies how states must handle child custody disputes when state laws are different or that sets out the process by which a person winning a lawsuit in one state can enforce the order in another state.

Article IV, Section 2, Paragraph 1

Section 2. The Citizens of each State shall be entitled to all Privileges and Immunities of Citizens in the several States.

The following continues with the Annenberg Classroom:

"Article IV, Section 2 guarantees that states cannot discriminate against citizens of other states. States must give people from other states the same fundamental rights it gives its own citizens. For example, Arizona cannot prohibit New Mexico residents from traveling, owning property, or working in Arizona, nor can the state impose substantially different taxes on residents and nonresidents. But certain distinctions between residents and nonresidents—such as giving state residents a right to buy a hunting license at a lower cost— are permitted.

"Article IV, Section 2 also establishes rules for when an alleged criminal flees to another state. It provides that the second state is obligated to return the fugitive to the state where the crime was committed. The process used to return fugitives (extradition) was first created by Congress and originally enforced by the governors of each state. Today courts enforce the return of accused prisoners. Fugitives do not need to have been charged with the crime in the first state in order to be captured in the second and sent back. Once returned, the state can charge the accused with any crime for which there is evidence.

"In contrast, when a foreign country returns a fugitive to a state for trial, the state is only allowed to try the fugitive on the charges named in the extradition papers (the formal, written request for the fugitive's return).

"The fugitives from labor provision gave slave owners a nearly absolute right to recapture runaway slaves who fled to another state, even if slavery was outlawed in that state. This also meant that state laws in free states intended to protect runaway slaves were unconstitutional because they interfered with the slave owner's right to the slave's return. The adoption of Amendment XIII, which abolishes slavery and prohibits involuntary servitude, nullified this provision.

Article IV, Section 2, Paragraph 2

A Person charged in any State with Treason, Felony, or other Crime, who shall flee from Justice and be found in another State, shall, on Demand of the executive Authority of the State from which he fled, be delivered up to be removed to the State having Jurisdiction of the Crime.

This paragraph has the same provisions as the previous one but specifically addresses treason and felonies. Treason and felonies are treated several times in the Constitution so the reader should again refer to Article I, Section 6, Paragraph 1 for a complete discussion.

Article IV, Section 2, Paragraph 3

> **No Person held to Service or Labour in one State, under the Laws thereof, escaping into another, shall, in Consequence of any Law or Regulation therein, be discharged from such Service or Labour, but shall be delivered up on Claim of the Party to whom such Service or Labour may be due.**

Again this paragraph addresses another aspect of different laws in different states, and specifically addresses slavery. Slavery was the big issue on which the Constitution would be adopted or not. This paragraph provided for slave owners to have their property returned to them if the slave is caught in another state. The reason the underground railroad was established all the way to Canada was to avoid the application of this paragraph. It was written to protect slave owners for only 20 years after the Constitution was ratified.

Article IV, Section 3, Paragraph 1

Section 3. New States may be admitted by the Congress into this Union; but no new State shall be formed or erected within the Jurisdiction of any other State; nor any State be formed by the Junction of two or more States, or Parts of States, without the Consent of the Legislatures of the States concerned as well as of the Congress.

These are the conditions of new states being added to the country. This provision has become very important in today's climate as factions within states are beginning to attempt to divide states along political and cultural lines. Currently rural areas within states are attempting to disassociate themselves from the urban areas because they feel they are no longer represented in the legislative bodies of their states. Colorado and California currently have groups attempting to separate rural areas from urban areas thus forming new states from parts of the same state. The problem for them is that the legislature that is ignoring the rural areas is the same legislature that must approve the division.

Here is an interesting part of United States History. During the Civil War, West Virginia was admitted into the Union as the 35th U.S. state.

In 1861, as the United States itself became massively divided over slavery, leading to the American Civil War (1861–1865), the western regions of Virginia split with the eastern portion politically, and the two were never reconciled as a single state again.

In April 1863, U.S. President Abraham Lincoln proclaimed the admission of West Virginia into the Union effective June 20, 1863. Therefore, as the procedure did not follow the Constitution, West Virginia might not legitimately be a State of the Union, but a mere illegal breakaway province of the Commonwealth of Virginia.

Article IV, Section 3, Paragraph 2

> **The Congress shall have Power to dispose of and make all needful Rules and Regulations respecting the Territory or other Property belonging to the United States; and nothing in this Constitution shall be so construed as to Prejudice any Claims of the United States, or of any particular State.**

This paragraph is used today to justify the federal government's control over so much land. But the phrase "Property belonging to the United States;" is the problem. You see according to Article I, Section 8, Paragraph 17 the only land belonging to the United States must meet certain rules and when the land meets those rules then they have power over it. Any land not meeting those rules is not the property of the United States to begin with and therefore this paragraph does not apply.

Article IV, Section 4

> **Section 4. The United States shall guarantee to every State in this Union a Republican Form of Government, and shall protect each of them against Invasion, and on Application of the Legislature, or of the Executive (when the Legislature cannot be convened), against domestic Violence.**

Our country is based on the Constitution and is not a democracy at all. We are a republic! A republic is a form of government where individuals are selected by the people to be their representatives in the government of a specific geographic area. This paragraph guarantees that every state will be a republic. It then goes on to place the responsibility of protection against invasion both from without or from within the state on the United States government when the official government of the state requests assistance.

The Northwest Ordinance, adopted July 13, 1787, by the Confederation Congress, chartered a government for the Northwest Territory, provided a method for admitting new states to the Union from the territory, and listed a bill of rights guaranteed in the territory. This Ordinance refers to the area that became the states of Ohio, Indiana, Illinois, Michigan, Wisconsin and a portion of Minnesota.

This ordinance laid the basis for the admission of its constituent parts as states into the union. It was written outlining the requirements of any territory being admitted to the Union of States, and the important part of this NW Ordinance is that religion was to be taught in the schools. Not any particular religion, but, as Jefferson called it, America's Religion, belief in God, and that God holds man accountable for his actions while on earth.

ARTICLE V

The Amendment Process

Article V, Paragraph 1

The Congress, whenever two thirds of both Houses shall deem it necessary, shall propose Amendments to this Constitution, or, on the Application of the Legislatures of two thirds of the several States, shall call a Convention for proposing Amendments, which, in either Case, shall be valid to all Intents, and Purposes, as Part of this Constitution, when ratified by the Legislatures of three fourths of the several States, or by Conventions in three fourths thereof, as the one or the other Mode of Ratification may be proposed by the Congress; Provided that no Amendment which may be made prior to the Year One thousand eight hundred and eight shall in any Manner affect the first and fourth Clauses in the Ninth Section of the first Article; and that no State, without its Consent, shall be deprived of its equal Suffrage in the Senate.

Find the word "or" in the Article. That word denotes different thoughts; like this or that. Notice the Article includes the word "or" twice and they seem to denote three different ways to amend the Constitution.

Reviewed the situation colonies that faced the delegates to the Constitutional Convention in 1787. Each of them represented an existing government that had authority over its portion of the new Americas. The delegates each guarded the autonomy of their State throughout the entire Convention.

In addition, there were individuals who were considered Federalists and others who were Anti-Federalists. The Federalists wanted a strong central government, and the Anti-federalists wanted strong State governments. These two factions were at odds with each other during and after the Constitutional Convention.

As they developed Article V it appears that they established three different ways to amend the Constitution.

- One was an amendment process that started in Congress with two thirds of both houses.
- Next they established a process that started in the states and went to Congress.

These two processes were separated by the word "or" and both of them were controlled by Congress even down to the ratification process with the words "as the one or the other Mode of Ratification may be proposed by the Congress" meaning conventions or legislatures of the states.

- Then, the Founders, probably influenced by the Anti-federalists, inserted another comma prior to the second "or" establishing a third amendment process using the words "by Conventions in three fourths thereof."

This established an amendment process outside of the authority of the federal government since it rested entirely with the states. This process was used in the ratification of the Constitution itself.

In the supreme court's decision on the case United States v Sprague (1931) concerning Article V the comma preceding the second "or" was omitted. That omission changed the entire original meaning of the Article. The change focused on the modes of ratification, rather than a completely separate ratification process providing more amendment power to the states. In other words, the court changed the Constitution's punctuation to establish their decision and that set a precedent that has dominated political thought ever since.

From George Washington's Farewell Address we read:

"The basis of our political Systems is the right of the people to make and to alter their Constitutions of Government. But the Constitution which at any time exists, 'till changed by an explicit and authentic act of the whole People, is sacredly obligatory upon all."

I believe that Washington meant that the "whole people" were in charge of the Constitution, and it was meant to stay that way. Without an amendment process outside of the federal government's control, his statement could not apply.

Finally, let's look at the last portion of the Article where the prohibitions are listed. The first prohibition established that "no Amendment which may be made prior to the Year One thousand eight hundred and eight shall in any Manner affect the first and fourth Clauses in the Ninth Section of the first Article." This prohibition was part of the Slavery issue. When the plantations were financed through the Bank of England the loans included some collateral of the value of the slaves. If the slaves were immediately freed, that collateral would disappear and the Bank of England would be able to foreclose on all of the plantations of the South. The delegates agreed that 20 years would be sufficient time for them to get these loans satisfied and the date of 1808 was agreed to. That was the reason for this prohibition.

The second prohibition, "no State, without its Consent, shall be deprived of its equal Suffrage in the Senate" was to protect State's representation in the new government. The Constitution was formed by two separate powers, the People and the States. The People's representatives were the representatives they elected for the House of Representatives, and the State's representatives were the Senators they appointed for the Senate. The Founders did not want to lose their representation in the federal government so they included a prohibition that would make any amendment removing that representation null and void. Enter the Seventeenth Amendment. It should never even have been proposed as it was unconstitutional even to consider it. If a State wanted to give up its right it could, but any amendment taking away their representation was illegal.

There is one other item that should be mentioned before we complete the discussion about Article V. That has to do with Black's Law Dictionary which is the dictionary for attorneys. In the portion of the definitions concerning amendments, it says that no amendment can alter a contract. An amendment can correct errors and add to the contract, but it cannot change the contract itself. Therefore, all amendments to the Constitution that change the basic document are null and void per the law of contracts. That includes amendments 11, 12, 14, 16, 17, 23, and 25 which all change the original document. It is interesting to note that these seven amendments are the amendments that are destroying our Republic. Repeal these amendments and most of the problems facing our nation would be resolved.

ARTICLE VI

The Supreme Law and Other Provisions

Article VI, Paragraph 1

>All Debts contracted and Engagements entered into, before the Adoption of this Constitution shall be as valid against the United States under this Constitution, as under the Confederation.

The Founders recognized that the current form of government had outstanding debts. This paragraph established the requirement that all current debts would be honored by the new government.

Article VI, Paragraph 2

>This Constitution, and the Laws of the United States which shall be made in Pursuance thereof, and all Treaties made, or which shall be made, under the Authority of the United States, shall be the supreme Law of the Land; and the Judges in every State shall be bound thereby, any Thing in the Constitution or Laws of any State to the Contrary notwithstanding.

Let's review this paragraph beginning with the words: "This Constitution, and the Laws of the United States which shall be made in Pursuance

135

thereof, and all Treaties made, or which shall be made, under the Authority of the United States, shall be the supreme Law of the Land;"

The first two words of this first phrase are "This Constitution" and these words establish the basic foundation. This means that the Constitution is the supreme law of the land, and all other items are subservient to it. All laws must be in accordance with the Constitution. If they are not, they are null and void! Then the second part of the basic foundation is established with the words "and the laws of the United States. But there is a qualifier concerning the laws of the United States. That qualifier is the requirement that the laws shall be made in accordance with the Constitution.

Have you heard the term nullification? In the context of the Constitution it means the States have the right to void any federal law that violates the Constitution or goes beyond the meaning of the Constitution. The Tenth Amendment insures that the States can do anything that is not reserved to the federal government except for those items covered in Article I, Section 10. Anytime the federal government exceeds the law of the Constitution the States have the right and responsibility to nullify that law or rule or opinion. This applies no matter which federal agency does it.

The next subject in this paragraph is to do with treaties and they are also qualified with the phrase "under the authority of the United States." What does the authority of the United States mean? It means that the treaties cannot violate the previous two foundations. In other words treaties must first be in accordance with the Constitution and second they must be in accordance with the proper laws of the United States. The treaties do not supersede the Constitution or the proper laws of the United States but are subservient to them.

The supreme court has interpreted this paragraph as saying that treaties supersede the Constitution. As anyone with a modicum of understanding would realize, the Founding Fathers did not intend that this paragraph be construed in this manner, but the "progressive" justices on the supreme court have done so.

The first such occurrence happened as early as 1796 in the case of Ware v Hylton. Even though this was in the same period of time as the Constitution was written there were individuals even then who were trying to usurp our rights. This case involved the taking of Hylton's property to fulfill a treaty with Great Britain. The treaty was upheld and he lost his property!

The next time an erroneous interpretation of this provision occurred was in 1920 in the case of Missouri v Holland. In this case the supreme court decided that the powers reserved to the States by the Tenth Amendment would be given to the national government by a treaty. What? The powers of the States taken away with a treaty? The supreme court was really off base in this case. The real question is why did the Congress not intervene and rule against this abuse of power by the supreme court?

Then, in 1942 the problem continues with the case of United States v Pink. The doctrine that treaties supersede the Constitution was extended to apply to executive agreements negotiated by the President. These agreements could be done by the President or by bureaucrats in the name of the President. They are not proper treaties and have not been approved by the Senate but could still supersede the Constitution per this decision. In this case the court held that a personal agreement between President Roosevelt and the Russian Prime Minister nullified provisions of the laws of the State of New York and of the American Constitution.

The supreme court is constantly changing the Constitution to be what they want it to be at any given moment. This court must have the least knowledge about the Constitution of any other government entity and they claim to have the final say on what it means. It is the supreme law of the land and it's too bad nobody knows what it says. It is not hard to read, we just need to do it.

Article VI, Paragraph 3

The Senators and Representatives before mentioned, and the Members of the several State Legislatures, and all executive and judicial Officers, both of the United States and of the several States, shall be bound by Oath or Affirmation, to support this Constitution; but no religious Test shall ever be required as a Qualification to any Office or public Trust under the United States.

This paragraph establishes the oath of office and today most politicians just think that is the biggest joke of all. These officials swear with their right arm raised to the square that they will support and defend the Constitution and in the same day, just a few hours later, will violate that oath! It has no meaning whatsoever in this day and age. They just laugh at it and destroy our rights willy-nilly with no regard of any personal honor. All of them with this attitude should be impeached immediately for constantly violating that oath.

The last part of this article speaks of a religious test. This prohibition of a religious test should be a no-brainier but it seems that even that is currently under fire. Christians are being punished for being Christians by the very people that have taken the Oath of Office. More total dishonesty!

Appendix 2 provides additional insight on the subject of treaties as intended by the Founding Fathers..

ARTICLE VII

Ratifying the Constitution

Article VII, Paragraph 1

The Ratification of the Conventions of nine States shall be sufficient for the Establishment of this Constitution between the States so ratifying the Same.

Look back at the third amendment process of Article V and you will see it borne out in this Article. This Article calls for State conventions IN nine States to ratify the Constitution These are not State legislative bodies but conventions specifically organized for the sole purpose of ratifying the Constitution.

Article VII, Paragraph 2

done in Convention by the Unanimous Consent of the States present, the Seventeenth Day of September in the Year of our Lord one thousand seven hundred and eighty seven, and of the Independence of the United States of America the Twelfth In Witness whereof We have hereunto subscribed our Names.

This is the summary of who consented to this Constitution including the official date. The document was then sent to the Congress and Congress sent it to the States for ratification. Each of them held a convention and sent back their ratification or their comments of what would be required for their ratification. I have copies of the documents that were sent to the States and the documents that were returned with their comments.

Signatures

Article VII is followed by the signatures of the delegates State by State.

**GEORGE WASHINGTON, President
and deputy from Virginia**

**New Hampshire   John Langdon
           Nicholas Gilman**

**Massachusetts   Nathaniel Gorham
           Rufus King**

**Connecticut   Wm. Saml. Johnson
           Roger Sherman**

New York   Alexander Hamilton

**New Jersey   Wil: Livingston
           David Brearley
           Wm. Paterson
           Jona: Dayton**

**Pennsylvania   B Franklin
           Thomas Mifflin
           Robt Morris
           Geo. Clymer
           Thos. FitzSimons
           Jared Ingersoll
           James Wilson**

Gouv Morris

Delaware   Geo: Read
          Gunning Bedford jun
          John Dickinson
          Richard Bassett
          Jaco: Broom

Maryland   James McHenry
          Daniel of St. Thos. Jenifer
          Danl Carroll

Virginia   John Blair
          James Madison Jr.

North Carolina Wm. Blount
          Richd. Dobbs Spaight
          Hu Williamson

South Carolina J. Rutledge
          Charles Cotesworth Pinckney
          Pierce Butler

Georgia   William Few
          Abr Baldwin

Attest. William Jackson, Secretary

(Rhode Island not present)

144

Amendments to the Constitution

Now let's move on to the amendments to the Constitution. Remember the legal requirements for amendments of a contract that were discussed in Article V. The Constitution is a contract between three powers: 1. the People, 2. the individual States, and 3. the United States government. Since the Constitution is a contract, these rules apply to all of the amendments. As you read the amendments you will see many that violate these rules by changing the words of the actual contract.

We often forget that the States were one of the two entities or powers that actually formed the government. If they had not agreed to this contract the United States government would not have been formed in the first place. In today's world, we forget that the States gave up SOME of their autonomy so that the United States government could be established. We now look at the States as inferior to the federal government, but that is not correct. The States are superior to the federal government as they gave it its power in the first place.

The first ten amendments are called the Bill of Rights because they specifically spelled out the

145

rights of the citizens in this new government. These rights are from God not the federal government! These are the rights pointed out in the Declaration of Independence. Unalienable rights means that these rights came from God, and government cannot take them away!

From Merriam-Webster Dictionary:

"vested right

"noun

"Legal Definition of *vested right:*

"A right belonging completely and unconditionally to a person as a property interest which cannot be impaired or taken away (as through retroactive legislation) without the consent of the owner

Vested rights are the God-given rights.

The following is from Lexrex.com. Lexrex is focused on helping the legal services industry.

"A Principle of The Traditional American Philosophy

"Unalienable Rights - From God

146

". . . endowed by their Creator with certain <u>unalienable rights</u> . . ." - Declaration of Independence

"The Principle

"The traditional American philosophy teaches that Man, The Individual, is endowed at birth with rights which are unalienable because given by his Creator.

"The Only Moral Basis

"This governmental philosophy is uniquely American. God-given rights are sometimes called Natural Rights--those possessed by man under the Laws of Nature, meaning under the laws of God's creation and therefore by gift of God. Man has no power to alienate, to dispose of, by surrender, barter or gift, his God-given rights, according to the American philosophy. This is the meaning of "unalienable".

"One underlying consideration is that for every such right there is a correlative, inseparable duty--for every aspect of freedom there is a corresponding responsibility; so that it is always Right-Duty and Freedom-

147

Responsibility, or Liberty-Responsibility. There is a duty, or responsibility, to God as the giver of these unalienable rights: a moral duty--to keep secure and use soundly these gifts, with due respect for the equal rights of others and for the right of Posterity to their just heritage of liberty. Since this moral duty cannot be surrendered, bartered, given away, abandoned, delegated or otherwise alienated, so is the inseparable right likewise unalienable. This concept of rights being unalienable is thus dependent upon belief in God as the giver. This indicates the basis and the soundness of Jefferson's statement (1796 letter to John Adams): "If ever the morals of a people could be made the basis of their own government it is our case" . . .

"Right, Reason, and Capacity to Be Self-governing

"For the security and enjoyment by Man of his Divinely created rights, it follows implicitly that Man is endowed by his Creator not only with the right to be self-governing but also with the capacity to reason and, therefore, with the capacity to be self-governing. This is implicit in the philosophy proclaimed in the Declaration of

Independence. Otherwise, Man's unalienable rights would be of little or no use or benefit to him. Faith in Man--in his capacity to be self-governing--is thus related to faith in God as his Creator, as the giver of these unalienable rights and this capacity.

"Rights--as Prohibitions Against Government

"Certain specific rights of The Individual are protected in the original Constitution but this is by way of statements "in reverse," by way of express prohibitions against government. The word "right" does not appear in the original instrument. This is because it was designed to express the grant by the people of specific, limited powers to the central government, created by them through this basic law, as well as certain specific limitations on its powers, and on the preexisting powers of the State governments, expressed as prohibitions of things forbidden. Every provision in it pertains to power.

The Constitution's first eight amendments list certain rights of The individual and prohibit the doing of certain things by the central, or Federal, government which, if done, would violate these rights. These amendments were intended by their Framers and Adopters merely to express a few of the already existing, implied prohibitions against the federal government only, supplementing the prohibitions previously specified expressly in the original Constitution and supplementing and confirming its general, over-all, implied, prohibition as to all things concerning which it withheld power from this government. Merely confirming expressly some of the already existing, implied prohibitions, these amendments did not create any new ones. They are, therefore, more properly referred to as a partial list of limitations on government. This hinges upon the uniquely American concepts stated in the Declaration of Independence: that Men, created of God, in turn create their governments and grant to them only "just" (limited) powers, primarily to make and keep secure their God-given, unalienable rights including, in part, the right to Life, Liberty and the pursuit of Happiness. Under the American philosophy and system of constitutionally limited government, "the people surrender nothing;" instead, they merely delegate to government, to public servants as public trustees, limited powers and therefore,they have no need of particular reservations (in a Bill of Rights). This is the basic reason why the Framing Convention omitted from the Constitution anything in the nature of a separate Bill of Rights, as being unnecessary.

An Endless List of Rights

"To attempt to name all of these rights, starting with "Life, Liberty and the pursuit of Happiness" mentioned in the Declaration of Independence, would be to start an endless list which would add up to the whole of Man's Freedom (Freedom from Government-over-Man). They would add up to the entirety of Individual Liberty (Liberty against Government-over-Man). Innumerable rights of the individual are embraced in the Ninth Amendment, which states: "The enumeration in the Constitution of certain rights shall not be construed to deny or disparage others retained by the people." Some idea of how vast the list would be is indicated by just one general freedom which leads into almost all of Free Man's activities of daily living throughout life: freedom of choice. This term stands for the right to do, and equally not to do, this or that, as conscience, whim or

151

judgment, taste or desire, of the individual may prompt from moment to moment, day by day, for as long as life lasts; but always, of course, with due regard for the equal rights of others and for the just laws expressive of the above-mentioned "just powers" of government designed to help safeguard the equal rights of all individuals. Spelled out in detail, this single freedom--freedom of choice--is almost all-embracing.

One of the rights not listed in the Constitution could be the Right to Exclude. This could be defined as the right to exclude anyone from your private property that you wanted to. For instance you could exclude all government officials at any level of government. This would keep petty inspectors, swat teams, the EPA, and other unconstitutional officials from disturbing you with unnecessary regulations and fines. America could be free again. This is just an idea.

Bill of Rights

First ten amendments to the Constitution

These amendments were added to insure that the federal government did not violate the inherent God-given rights that a person should enjoy. Those individuals who were against these amendments felt that the Constitution had already covered them. Today it is constantly demonstrated that the Constitution did not cover these rights adequately. It has turned out that they were actually quite necessary as the government has gone to great lengths to destroy them.

In today's world almost all of our rights have been either effectively altered or ignored completely. It is necessary for us to understand the rights in the Bill of Rights and their importance in order to know when the government is violating them.

First Amendment

Congress shall make no law respecting an establishment of religion, or prohibiting the free exercise thereof; or abridging the freedom of speech, or of the press; or the right of the people peaceably to assemble, and to petition the Government for a redress of grievances.

To begin with let's look at the specific freedoms and the rights included in this amendment. There are four specific freedoms and two rights covered. The freedoms are:

- freedom to establish a religion
- the freedom to exercise the beliefs of that religion
- freedom of speech and
- freedom of the press

The two rights are:

- to peacefully assemble and
- to petition the government for redress of a grievance.

It would seem that these 45 words would be easy to understand, but the supreme court can't seem to be able to do it.

Freedom to Establish or Exercise a Religion

The first 10 words are: "Congress shall make no law respecting an establishment of religion." Very clear but not understandable in today's society.

In the Colonial Era governments regularly established a national religion. Eventually, everyone was required to belong to that religion with a penalty of prison and torture for not joining. The Founders did not want a compulsory national religion.

Here is a quote that is of interest:

"It's impossible to have religious freedom in any nation where churches are licensed to the government." - Congressman George Hansen

In spite of the First Amendment, and the above quote, Senator Lyndon B. Johnson decided to silence the political activities and the influence of the churches. He underhandedly did this by introducing and passing a bill that said, if all churches would organize as 501(c)(3) organizations they would not have to pay income taxes. But, prior to that bill they didn't have to pay taxes anyway. He convinced the people into believing that since there was no current law to protect the churches they might have to pay taxes in the future so let's protect them them now.

Because of the 501(c)(3) requirement, churches no longer have religious freedom. Most churches in America have organized as "501(c)(3) tax-exempt religious organizations." This is a fairly recent trend that has only been going on for about fifty years. Churches were only added to section 501(c)(3) of the tax code in 1954. We can thank Sen. Lyndon B. Johnson for that. Johnson was no ally of the churches. As part of his political agenda, Johnson had it in his mind to silence the churches and eliminate the significant influence the churches had always had on shaping "public policy."

Although Johnson proffered this as a "favor" to churches, the favor also came with strings attached (more like shackles). One need not look far to see the devastating effects 501(c)(3) acceptance has had to the churches, and the consequent restrictions placed upon any 501(c)(3) church. 501(c)(3) churches are prohibited from addressing, in any tangible way, the vital issues of the day.

If 501(c)(3) churches openly speak out, or organize in opposition to, anything that the government declares "legal," even if it is immoral (e.g. abortion, homosexuality, etc.), they will jeopardize their tax-exempt status. The 501(c)(3) requirement has had a "chilling effect" upon the free speech rights of churches. LBJ was a shrewd and cunning politician who seemed to well-appreciate how easily many of the clergy would sell out.

Did churches ever need to seek permission from the government to be exempt from taxes? Were churches prior to 1954 taxable? No, churches have never been taxable. To be taxable churches would first need to be under the jurisdiction, and therefore under the taxing authority, of the government. The First Amendment clearly places churches outside the jurisdiction of the civil government: "Congress shall make no law respecting an establishment of religion, nor prohibiting the free exercise thereof."

As a matter of interest in 1954, at President Dwight D. Eisenhower's urging, the Congress also legislated that "under God" be added to the Pledge of Allegiance, making the Pledge read:

I pledge allegiance to the flag of the United States of America and to the Republic for which it stands, one nation under God, indivisible, with liberty and justice for all.

What's going on here? One hand giveth and the

other taketh away. Sometime during this same period, churches began the custom of not discussing politics in their classes or environments. And the people at large began the custom of not discussing either politics or religion. This custom was probably established because these two subjects can sometimes cause heated debates. But what has really happened with this total picture?

The pulpit was a major factor during the Revolutionary War. It was often referred to as the Black Regiment. This was because the ministers mostly wore black robes when they delivered their sermons. These ministers were the backbone of the revolution as they taught the people. Where is the Black Regiment of today when we need it so badly? It has been gagged by the 501(c)(3) paragraph of the IRS code which officially says churches are not taxable. But by extension it also says that donations to these organizations are also not taxable and there is the rub.

And that's just one part of the issue with these 16 words. Next let's look at religion in schools. No child has any freedom of religion in any public school. These are the four major cases that have destroyed these freedoms

- 1- Brown v Education 1954,

- 2- Cooper v Aaron 1959,
- 3- Engel v Vitale 1962,
- and 4- Abington School District v Schempp 1963.

Because of the nefarious activities of the supreme court with these four cases all Christian religious activities are completely illegal. A teacher or a student cannot even have a Bible in his possession. In spite of the First Amendment freedom of religion is banded from all public schools. They cannot even teach morals because that is defined as religion.

The next step was to eliminate all religion from any public square. No nativity scenes are allowed. The phrase Merry Christmas is being replaced with Happy Holidays. No Christmas carols can be sung in any public government location. No prayers can be offered at any public venue, except of course at the beginning of the sessions in Congress and at the supreme court.

No, there is no freedom of religion in our country any longer, except in private gatherings. And if the government can figure out how to do it, that will also be eliminated.

Freedom of Speech

This right is also on the chopping block. The term used to deny freedom of speech is "politically correct." Nothing can be said that is not politically correct. Most universities in our country control all speech. There are safe spaces on these university campuses, but these are reserved for people who want to get away from others. There are no conservative speeches or talks or opinions in class or any place on many campuses. Riots start when anyone tries to express a different point of view, and the school upholds the rioters. Students have been expelled from classes and have been denied graduation because they said something that was contrary to the current proper opinions of the day.

There is a whole list of names that are required to refer to gender and if you violate any of them you will be punished. Freedom of speech is not allowed in many situations today.

Additionally, there are those who allege that we must have laws against hate speech. What is hate speech all about. This is a type of speech that targets a certain category of people. But does the right of free speech come from the government? Can the government legally outlaw speech it doesn't like? No! Free speech predates the government and is an unalienable right. The concept of freedom of speech must allow speech that is uncomfortable to hear as well as speech that is comfortable. If we outlaw speech we don't like, then freedom of speech is lost for everybody.

There are types of speech that are not covered by freedom of speech. Those would be items like yelling fire in a crowded theater, or speech that effects national security, or speech that causes actual physical harm to someone. For example, freedom of speech ends at the tip of my nose. Hate speech does not physically harm someone; therefore a law cannot be passed outlawing it if we are to remain a free country.

Freedom of the Press

Freedom of the press is a fundamental right. But currently the press has begun to use this by violating the rights of others. Then, since most of the press is behind all of the nonsense, individual journalists don't want to make waves. So to keep their jobs and influence they don't violate the established norms. If one were to do so, he would have to find another type of job because he wouldn't survive. An interesting part of this attitude of the press, is that you can say any vile, viscous, degrading, or insulting phrase as long as it is directed at the current politician that is not in favor.

Then in 1964 the supreme court in its wisdom decided that the media can lie if it so chooses. This was done with the decision in the case New York Times Company v Sullivan. Since that decision the press has been free to print or say anything it wants about anyone it wants without fear of it being against the law as long as it is not done with malicious intent. That was the birth of the "fake news" that we hear so much of today. Honest journalism is dead in America.

Right of the People to Peacefully Assemble

"The right of the people peaceably to assemble" is also under fire. There are communities where people are forbidden to assemble for religious purposes. These cases are brought to the attention of the civil government by their own neighbors. Then the individuals who are assembling are punished. Yes, the right of assembly is also being destroyed. We are in a society that can no longer tolerate a difference of opinion of any sort in any manner. These are selfish people who can't tolerate other points of view, and the government is enforcing their crybaby attitudes.

The Right to Petition the Government

"The right to petition the government for a redress of grievances" still seems to be a part of our society.

163

But when you contact your congressman or senator with a gripe and a request for redress, what do you get? You get a ready made form letter that sits on a shelf ready to mail out. This letter doesn't really say anything, it's sent to placate you. Are you really being heard? Not likely! The government basically doesn't really pay any attention. But given the current direction of our society even this right could be gone at any moment.

Second Amendment

A well regulated Militia, being necessary to the security of a free State, the right of the people to keep and bear Arms, shall not be infringed.

In the discussion of the militia in Article I, Section 8, Paragraph 15 and 16 we found that the federal government was responsible for arming this organization, which is composed of regular people. There are actually people who are attempting to revoke this amendment. Interesting that this is the only amendment that is covered in detail in the Constitution itself and that detail is found in Article I, Section 8. This amendment is actually redundant, but the Founders wanted additional protection against possible tyranny of the central government. This amendment is actually very clear.

What did the Founders say? They said that the American people have a collective right to protect themselves against the evil of standing armies by forming a general militia composed of all the people. That is: *A well-regulated militia being necessary to the security of a free state. . . .*

What does the word "state" mean in this amendment? When the Constitution was written the word state meant New York, Virginia, or Connecticut. Today it also includes Idaho, Iowa, and Ohio. Therefore this amendment means that each state must have a militia for its security. Since every able bodied man will be in this militia each state will have a significant military force.

What type of arms do you think the Founders meant? It stands to reason that they meant the arms of their day. Just like the British had when they fought in the Revolutionary War, the most up to date available. Therefore, that is what they intended for the militia both in this reference and in Article I, Section 8, paragraph 16. The government should be providing the most up to date weapons available.

In addition, the Founders said that American citizens have an individual and inviolable right to arm themselves to protect their lives, liberty, and property: *the right of the people to keep and bear arms shall not be infringed.*

The purpose of the militia is to keep the central government under control if necessary.

Third Amendment

No soldier shall, in time of peace be quartered in any house, without the consent of the Owner, nor in time of war, but in a manner to be prescribed by law.

We find two rights listed here. Soldiers shall not be housed in a private citizens home, without his consent during peace time nor during war.

Prior to the Revolutionary War, British troops were often housed in the homes of the colonists. This was so offensive that a right was listed to insure that the federal government would not abuse the private property of the citizens of the country. This is one of only three places that private property rights are discussed.

Private property rights are a must to a free country. Without private property there is no liberty. If the government can tell you how to use your private property, liberty is lost. What are some of the ways that private property is abused in today's world?

- Minimum Wages. Neither businesses nor individuals can decide what to receive or pay workers for their services. Your labor is a part of your private property and if the government

167

controls or regulates how you use it, you have lost your personal private property rights. Businesses also have private property rights and they should be able to control what they pay their employees. If the government dictates that they pay too little they have lost that property right. In fact many business have gone out of business completely because they cannot afford the minimum wage requirement. In that case the government has actually stolen their business from them.. If the worker feels the pay is too low they can easily quit and find another job.

- Zoning Regulations. Both government and Homeowners Associations (HOA), control how you can use your personal property. This means you lose your right to use your private property as you see fit.
- Licensing. Many states require licenses to work in certain fields. The rules for licensing usually include difficult and expensive unimportant items. The result is that you often cannot qualify to work in the field you choose. These licensing procedures are often, if not almost always, encouraged by the businesses that are already operating in the field, with the actual intention of keeping competition out. These licensing procedures often cause a loss of your opportunity to use your personal labor

and therefore a loss of your personal private property.

- Property Tax. This is usually a local tax used to support schools, but it's main result is to keep your home and property under the control of the local government. Think of it this way. If you do not pay your property tax, what happens to your private property that you have already purchased and own outright? The local government confiscates your property and sells it for taxes. Property taxes are continually raised, eventually to levels you cannot afford to pay, and the home you have lived in for your entire life is taken from you by the government and sold. To avoid this, you must sell it and abandon your memories and security. This is legal theft of your private property.

- Single Family Homes. (includes no businesses) In fact this is a form of zoning. This concept controls the use of your property. If you have an extra room and want to rent it out you are prevented from doing it by government. In the past you could live in the same building as your business. Today there are zoning laws that prevent that. They have no right to tell you how to use your space.

- Control of Interest Rates. This is quite an obscure control of your property. This allows the government to control what you can buy with your money. Most people don't realize that interest rates are arbitrarily set by the Federal Reserve. The Federal Reserve does not follow market directions it creates them. It uses the excuse that increases or decreases of interest rates helps the economy. In actual fact higher interest rates either prevent or delay your opportunity to make some purchases. In this way your private property, your income, is controlled by the government for its own purposes.

- Subsidies. These are tax breaks or outright payments to certain sectors of the community. If you are making or buying an item selected by the government as important, the government will pay you for doing it. This gives you an advantage over the other parts of the economy, and therefore hurts the use of the private property of those not in favor.
- Income Taxes. This is completely unconstitutional and always favors certain sectors of the economy. It takes your money (your private property) and gives it to someone else who didn't earn it. All income tax provisions hurt someone to provide for someone else.

Fourth Amendment

The right of the people to be secure in their persons, houses, papers, and effects against unreasonable searches and seizures, shall not be violated, and no Warrants shall issue, but upon probable cause, supported by Oath or affirmation, and particularly describing the place to be searched, and the persons or things to be seized.

This amendment could be divided to show the following rights. It is also possible to divide it further and designate more than the four I have designated.

1. The right of the people to be secure in their persons, houses, papers, and effects.
2. The right against unreasonable searches and seizures.
3. The right protecting citizens from improper warrants unless there is probable cause, supported by Oath or affirmation,
4. The right that the warrant must describe particularly the place to be searched, and the persons or things to be seized.

We find here another provision protecting private property. It prevents government from forcing their way into your home, car, and body without probable cause. This protects you from government overreach or harassment. It also limits what the government can do when it enters your private property in the process.

Now let's review a law of the State of California. This state seems to have a goal of destroying the basic liberties of its citizens and setting precedences that other states could follow. The following article is an example of this. California has passed a law that clearly violates the Fourth Amendment.

California Sued for Keeping DNA of Innocent People

World Net Daily
December 16, 2018

"There is no legitimate interest in retaining samples from people who have no felony convictions

"One-third of people arrested for felonies in California are never convicted," explained Marcy Darnovsky of the Center for Genetics.

"The government has no legitimate interest in retaining DNA samples and

172

profiles from people who have no felony convictions, and it's unconstitutional for the state to hold on to such sensitive material without any finding of guilt," she said.

"California long has collected DNA from people convicted of felonies. In 2009, the state began requiring DNA collection for anyone charged with a felony, including those later determined to be innocent.

"Giving a DNA sample is not optional. Refusal can be punished by a year in prison, and officers are authorized to use "physical force" to obtain a sample. "The intimate details that can be revealed by a person's DNA only increases as technology develops, exposing plaintiffs to ever heightening degrees of intrusiveness," EFF (Electronic Frontier Foundation) said. "After collection, the DNA is analyzed and uploaded to the nationwide Combined DNA Index System, or 'CODIS,' which is shared with law enforcement across the U.S."

"One problem is that cases have shown DNA samples can implicate innocent people for crimes, "ranging from crime-lab sample mix-ups and sample contamination by forensic collectors, to subjective misreading of complex mixtures containing genetic material from multiple donors, to selective presentation of the evidence to juries."

"Racial profiling is another problem, the critics say.

"The failure to promptly expunge profiles of innocent arrestees exploits and reinforces systemic racial and socio-economic biases," said Lisa Holder of the Equal Justice Society. "We want the court to recognize that California's DNA collection and retention practices are unfairly putting already vulnerable poor communities and people of color at even greater risk of racial profiling and law enforcement abuse."

"While the state allows people who are not convicted to request that their records be expunged, it is a lengthy process with uncertain results.

"An estimated 750,000 people qualify for that program, but only about 1,300 have been successful with their requests, EFF said.

"The indefinite retention of thousands of DNA profiles from people who are acquitted or never charged violates the California Constitution, and the Fourth Amendment of the United States Constitution, which affords both a right to privacy and a right against unlawful searches and seizures that are specifically aimed at protecting people from the government's overbroad retention of personal information," said EFF.

"Our DNA contains our entire genetic makeup – private and intensely personal information that maps who we are and where we come from," noted EFF lawyer Jamie Lee Williams. "It's time for the state to start honoring the privacy rights guaranteed to all Californians."

Fifth Amendment

No person shall be held to answer for a capital, or otherwise infamous crime, unless on a presentment or indictment of a Grand Jury, except in cases arising in the land or naval forces, or in the Militia, when in actual service in time of War or public danger; nor shall any person be subject for the same offence to be twice put in jeopardy of life or limb; nor shall be compelled in any criminal case to be a witness against himself, nor be deprived of life, liberty, or property, without due process of law; nor shall private property be taken for public use, without just compensation.

The intent in this paragraph is to protect the innocent and prevent repeated trials for the same offense. There are five specific rights or protections listed.

1. Indictment by a Grand Jury.
2. No person shall be subject twice for the same offense.
3. No person shall be compelled in any criminal case to be a witness against himself.
4. No person shall be deprived of life, liberty, or property, without due process of law.
5. No person's private property can be taken for public use, without just compensation.

Notice the two phrases "put in jeopardy of life" and "nor be deprived of life, liberty, or property, without due process of law." Obviously, the Framers considered that criminals could be deprived of life as long as due process of the law was followed. Capital punishment was a part of the Founder's society and they considered it a normal possibility.

The supreme court was at it again in 1922. The Fifth Amendment, as originally written in the Constitution, prohibits double jeopardy or prosecution for the same offense twice and doesn't provide for any exceptions. But in the wisdom of the supreme court they again found an exception that was never intended by the Founding Fathers. It is interesting that the supreme court continually finds new things any time they want to. They call this one the separate sovereign exception, and it was introduced in the 1922 Supreme Court case of US v Lanza.

That exception, which was created out of thin air, simply establishes that two separate government entities with the same law on both of their books can punish an individual for violating each separate law. This decision completely undermines the right and protection of this amendment by allowing each entity to punish the individual for exactly the same crime with independent punishments. Each state and the federal government are all considered different "sovereigns."

The decision is actually written as follows:

> "When the same act is an offense against both state and federal governments, its prosecution and punishment by the latter, after prosecution and punishment by the former, is not double jeopardy within the Fifth Amendment. P. 260 U. S. 382.

They consider:

> "An act denounced as a crime by both national and state sovereignties is an offense against the peace and dignity of both and may be punished by each.

Let's take a moment and examine the words alleging that the government cannot take your property without just compensation. First, what does the word "take" include? In Lucas v South Carolina Coastal Council, 505 U.S. 1003 (1992), the court held that where regulations completely deprive an owner of "all economically beneficial use" of his or her property, the government must pay just compensation. That means the government must completely take your property. If it allows you some continued use, then no compensation is required.

What does" just compensation" mean? U.S. supreme court decisions have all but eliminated "just compensation" except in the case of a complete taking of the use of the property. But what really is "just compensation." The government will use its immense power to pay you as little as possible. That's what "just compensation" actually means.

Now what does "for public use" mean? Most of us take that to mean government buildings, roads, parks or anything that the public would use. But after Kelo v The City of New London (2005) the court has essentially included a greater tax base as better public use. That means the government is now allowed to take your private property if the tax income for the new use is greater than the tax income that you provide. These are some of the ways that the Constitution has been corrupted.

Sixth Amendment

In all criminal prosecutions, the accused shall enjoy the right to a speedy and public trial, by an impartial jury of the State and district wherein the crime shall have been committed, which district shall have been previously ascertained by law, and to be informed of the nature and cause of the accusation; to be confronted with the witnesses against him; to have compulsory process for obtaining witnesses in his favor, and to have the assistance of counsel for his defense.

Here we find an additional six rights established. These are:

1. The right to a speedy and public trial.
2. The right for an impartial jury.
3. The right to be informed of the nature of the accusation.
4. The right to be confronted by the witnesses against him.
5. The right to compel witnesses for him to appear.
6. The right to counsel.

These rights are really self explanatory, but do we really have them? For example the right to a speedy trial is almost non-existent. This amendment is about criminal trials. There are so many people in the legal system that it is completely bogged down. Trials can go on for months as attorneys constantly push for more time to do their cases. The cost of all of these trials grows as they take longer and longer to finish.

Then, even after the trial ends the appeal process drags on for additional months. In some rare cases the criminal is in jail for so long just to get the trial finished, that he has served most or all of the punishment that the judge decrees.

Then what about impartial juries? First, the media publicizes the cases so completely they often convict the accused before the trial even starts. There is so much publicity that every possible juror has an opinion before he ever gets to court. How can an intelligent and impartial jury ever be selected? It is sometimes alleged that only the most ill-informed people ever serve on a jury.

The right to counsel is suspect. Sure the court will appoint one if you can't afford one, but what will be the quality of his representation? The law is so complicated and there are so many loopholes that many guilty individuals are never punished. The quality of your trial whether you are innocent or guilty could depend on how much money you have.

The other three rights are probably provided most of the time.

Seventh Amendment

In Suits at common law, where the value in controversy shall exceed twenty dollars, the right of trial by jury shall be preserved, and no fact tried by a jury, shall be otherwise re-examined in any Court of the United Sates than according to the rules of the common law.

What does "Suits at common law" mean? In the colonial era, suits at common law were non criminal cases. In today's society we call non-criminal cases civil cases. Therefore this amendment covers civil cases as opposed to the Sixth Amendment which covers criminal cases.

Again we have two rights in civil cases including:

1. The right to a trial by jury.

2. The right that a civil case will be treated as a civil case in any court in the United States.

There is another item worth noting to do with common law. Usually you will find the term common law in conjunction with code law. In this case, common law means civil law.

Code law changes based on the opinions of those judges on a particular day and those opinions can then change from year to year. Code law is always changing while common law or natural law never changes.

It appears that the distinguishing difference are the words "Suits at." Therefore it could be said that "Suits at common law" means civil cases while the term common law without the words "Suits at" means natural law.

What is the significance of the words: "where the value in controversy shall exceed twenty dollars?" This establishes an injury and a victim. Without a victim and a loss there is no crime, therefore, there would be no case for the court to decide. See the discussion in Appendix 1 Admiralty or Maritime Jurisdiction.

Eighth Amendment

Excessive bail shall not be required, nor excessive fines imposed, nor cruel and unusual punishment inflicted.

Here are three rights:

1. The right that bail will not be excessive.
2. The right limiting excessive fines.
3. The right against cruel and unusual punishment.

What might be considered excessive bail?

Bail is considered "excessive" when it is set at a figure higher than an amount which would be reasonably arrived at based on the situation and the type of offense.

Then what is an excessive fine?

The amount of the forfeiture must bear some relationship to the gravity of the offense that it is designed to punish.

The framers did not define what they meant by excessive bail or fines, so it has been left up to the courts to decide what is excessive. This allows a grab bag type of definition. The judge at the time decides what is excessive and it might not be impartial. There is recourse to a higher court and but that in itself incurs more time and additional costs. This is a nebulous situation.

What is cruel and unusual punishment? This term was used by our Founders to prohibit unreasonable torture such as disemboweling and mutilation. At the time the Constitution was being written these punishments were prevalent in Europe and England where kings and governments would use these tactics to make examples of political enemies or coerce men and women into confessions that often times were not true.

The supreme court began changing the original meaning of this amendment in 1972 with the Furman v Georgia case. In this case the court decided that three different men who had been sentenced to death by Georgia were subjected to a cruel and unusual punishment. So the first step in changing the Constitution was accomplished.

Furman was convicted of rape and murder. The penalty assigned for the conviction was the death penalty and it was set aside. Shouldn't we consider the terror the victim underwent during the commission of this crime? She was terribly abused and murdered. Here we are in essence saying that the right of the criminal is greater than the right of the victim. There is also another factor present here. If a criminal knows he cannot be executed for his actions, will he care as much about his actions? Punishments should be designed to deter crime. Another important factor is that the killing of a witness insures that the witness will not appear against the criminal. So in this case after the criminal raped the girl, he killed her to keep her silent. Who really suffered the cruel and unusual punishment?

Then the supreme court found in Roper v Simmons (2005) that imposing the death penalty on persons younger than 18 years old is also a violation of the Eighth Amendment. And then in Miller v Alabama, (2012), the court also held that mandatory sentences of life without the possibility of parole for juveniles is also cruel and unusual punishment. No consideration for the lives or futures of the victims is ever even considered.

Notice how the supreme court changes the meaning of the Constitution by deciding that the customs of today's society should replace what the Founders actually meant.

Ninth Amendment

The enumeration in the Constitution, of certain rights, shall not be constructed to deny or disparage others retained by the people.

Twenty-seven rights have been established by the Bill of Rights. That is not a complete listing of all of the possible rights. As was discussed during the introduction to the Bill of Rights, there is no way to list all of the possible rights we enjoy as citizens of the United States. Therefore, this amendment insures that other possible rights are included even though they are not listed in the Bill of Rights.

This amendment specifically states that the certain listed rights do not preclude others that are also retained by the people.

Our rights are from God and they are not limited. But we must also consider that some are calling for rights that really are not rights at all. For example there can be no such thing as freedom from poverty or hunger. It is not economically possible. They are not rights they are conditions of life.

Tenth Amendment

The powers not delegated to the United States by the Constitution, nor prohibited by it to the States, are reserved to the States respectively, or to the people.

This final amendment guaranteed that everything that is not granted to the federal government by this Constitution is reserved to the States unless the Constitution prohibited the States from doing it.

This is the catch all amendment insuring that the federal government cannot take over the States. The States were one of the two powers that created this document. The other power is the people themselves. The States and the people are in charge of the federal government, not the other way around.

In our current society the federal government has, in violation of this Constitution, taken over both the States and the people. We must get our autonomy back, and the only way that can be done is by reading and understanding the Constitution itself. That is the reason that this book was written.

Let's take a minute and review the actual power of the Tenth Amendment. Refer to pages 135 to 139 which covers Article VI. Think of what it means to the states if properly upheld. All state government officials take an oath to uphold the Constitution. This means that they are obligated to enforce the Constitution if it is violated by any state law or any federal action.

Remember all states are sovereign entities and as such should govern themselves. The supreme court unconstitutionally usurped the powers of the states in their decision on the case of Martin v Hunter in 1816.

With the responsibility of sovereignty what should the states do? First organize and arm a militia per Article I, Section 8, paragraphs 15 and 16 and the Second Amendment. Then using the powers given the states in Article VI begin nullifying any action of the federal government that is unconstitutional. This power is supported by the Tenth Amendment. All federal courts are governed by and cannot exceed the power delegated to them by Article III.

States, you have the power to begin putting our country back in its original proper direction. BEGIN USING IT.

These first ten amendments were ratified by the people of the United States effective December 15, 1791.

Eleventh to Twenty-Seventh Amendments To The Constitution

Eleventh Amendment

The Judicial power of the United States shall not be construed to extend to any suit in law or equity, commenced or prosecuted against one of the United States by Citizens of another State or by Citizens or Subjects of any Foreign State.

The following is from the Annenberg Classroom:

"**Eleventh Amendment - The Meaning**
After the U.S. Supreme Court ruled in 1793 that two South Carolina men could sue and collect debts from the State of Georgia, states-rights advocates in Congress and the states pushed for what became the Eleventh Amendment in 1795. The amendment specifically prohibits federal courts from hearing cases in which a state is sued by an individual from another state or another country. Protecting states from certain types

of legal liability is a concept known as "sovereign immunity."

"The amendment did not bar all lawsuits against states in federal courts. For example, as initially interpreted, the Eleventh Amendment did not bar suits against states when a matter of federal law was at issue nor did it prevent suits brought against a state by its own citizens. But more recently, a divided Supreme Court has held that states are immune from all lawsuits in federal courts unless they specifically agree to be sued.

Originally the supreme court was expected to deal with cases of the following nature, as established in Article III, Section 2, Paragraph 1.

1. between a State and Citizens of another State;
2. between a State, or the Citizens thereof, and foreign States, Citizens, or Subjects.

The Constitution gave the supreme court only eight powers, and this amendment removed one of those powers and part of another. The major change was that the supreme court could no longer review cases against the States to do with foreign powers or citizens from different States. As mentioned above in the case in 1793 the supreme court found for individuals against the state of Georgia. That was unacceptable to the States, so they banded together and removed that power. Now all States are immune from suits of citizens and foreign powers in federal courts.

It is interesting that the States did not want to apply the Bill of Rights to themselves during these early time periods, even though they wanted the federal government to follow it. This amendment established a basis that allowed the States to ignore the Bill of Rights.

As this amendment changes the wording of Article III, Section 2, Paragraph 1 of the Constitution. Therefore, it is illegal and null and void according to the definition of an amendment as shown in Black's Law Dictionary as we discussed earlier.

The Eleventh Amendment was ratified February 7, 1795.

Twelfth Amendment

The Electors shall meet in their respective states, and vote by ballot for President and Vice-President, one of whom, at least, shall not be an inhabitant of the same state with themselves; they shall name in their ballots the person voted for as President, and in distinct ballots the person voted for as Vice-President, and they shall make distinct lists of all persons voted for as President, and of all persons voted for as Vice-President, and of the number of votes for each, which lists they shall sign and certify, and transmit sealed to the seat of the government of the United States, directed to the President of the Senate;-The President of the Senate shall, in the presence of the Senate and House of Representatives, open all the certificates and the votes shall then be counted;-The person having the greatest number of votes for President, shall be the President, if such number be a majority of the whole number of Electors appointed; and if no person have such majority, then from the persons having the highest numbers not exceeding three on the list of those voted for as President, the House of Representatives shall choose immediately, by ballot, the President. But in choosing the President, the votes shall be taken by states, the representation from each state having one vote; a quorum for this purpose shall consist of a member or members from two-thirds of the states, and a majority of all the states shall be necessary to a choice. And if the House of Representatives shall not choose a President whenever the right of choice shall devolve upon them, before the fourth day of March next following, then the Vice-President shall act as President, as in the case of the death or other constitutional disability of the President. The person having the greatest number of votes as Vice-President, shall be the Vice-President, if such number be a majority of the whole number of Electors appointed, and if no person have a majority, then from the two highest numbers on the list, the Senate shall choose the Vice-President; a quorum for the purpose shall consist of two-thirds of the whole number of Senators, and a majority of the whole number shall be necessary to a choice. But no person constitutionally ineligible to the office of President shall be eligible to that of Vice-President of the United States.

This amendment is very long and very few people ever review it. But in spite of its length, it really does only one thing. It changes the requirement of Electoral College members to nominate one person for President and one person for Vice-President instead of two people for President.

It appears that the goal of this amendment is to get a two party system officially going. The amendment was ratified in 1804, but the two party system was already in motion. That system of voting for party candidates for the President was in place during the election of 1800. This amendment just solidified that change. In actual fact, the Electoral College has only functioned twice as intended in the entire history of the United States, these occurred during the two elections of George Washington.

The concept of the Electoral College has been kept in place, but its purpose has changed to just a mirror of the popular vote. Its real purpose is to nominate candidates for president. Then their nominations are tabulated by the State and forwarded to the Senate for a complete tabulation. They do not meet in one place and mirror the popular vote. They actually have a function, as **we are a Republic!**

Another important factor is that this amendment did not change the requirements of the Electoral College to nominate two individuals for president and no amendment ever has. Therefore, with regards to the election of the President, we have just ignored the Constitution throughout the entire history of our nation during the 1800s, the 1900s, and the 2000s.

One more very important fact is that this amendment, just like the Eleventh Amendment, changes the Constitution and as Black's Law Dictionary states, an amendment cannot change the wording of a contract. Therefore this amendment is also null and void according to the law.

The twelfth Amendment was Ratified June 15, 1804.

Thirteenth Amendment

Thirteenth Amendment, Section 1

> **Section 1. Neither slavery nor involuntary servitude, except as a punishment for crime whereof the party shall have been duly convicted, shall exist within the United Sates, or any place subject to their jurisdiction.**

What does "involuntary servitude" mean? It is a condition where men and women are forced into labor. The key word is involuntary. That could be likened to a concentration camp where people are forced into some type of work. It would also include a compulsory draft into the Armed Forces of this country or a requirement to serve in the Peace Corps or something like that. Both of these forced situations have been requirements at one time or another in our country.

Read that paragraph again. Have any of those draftees or Peace Corps workers ever been convicted of a crime? No. Yet they are forced by the federal government to work for the state without due process of law. This is precisely what "involuntary servitude" actually means.

What else falls involuntary servitude? Forced direct taxes on the people. The Sixteenth Amendment can be nullified by this amendment which predates it. Today direct taxes on the people takes over one-third of their income. We are forced by this amendment to work for the government clear into May before we begin to work for ourselves. We are in essence slaves for one-third of the year.

Thirteenth Amendment, Section 2

Section 2. Congress shall have power to enforce this article by appropriation legislation.

This paragraph gives the Congress the power to insure that the citizens of our country are not forced into "involuntary servitude." Yet we still have had the draft into the armed forces.

The Thirteenth Amendment was ratified December 6, 1865.

Fourteenth Amendment

Fourteenth Amendment, Section 1

> **Section 1. All persons born or naturalized in the United States and subject to the jurisdiction thereof, are citizens of the United States and of the State wherein they reside. No State shall make or enforce any law which shall abridge the privileges or immunities of citizens of the United States; nor shall any State deprive any person of life, liberty, or property; without due process of law; nor deny to any person within its jurisdiction the equal protection of the laws.**

This amendment has been misused over and over by individuals with a personal agenda. In almost all cases, these people ignore the wording of the amendment if it does not suit their purpose. It was written to ensure that the Southern States did not exclude the black race or anyone else from being considered as full citizens of the United States and denied voting privileges. Each section treats different aspects during the aftermath of the Civil War.

The key phrase in the first section concerning children born in this country is "subject to the jurisdiction thereof." There are two conditions included in this section and both must be met. Congressman Steven King of the 4th District of Iowa explains it very clearly as follows:

> "The plain meaning of the Fourteenth Amendment means that one must BOTH be born in United States AND be subject to the jurisdiction thereof. Since there are two explicit requirements, they both cannot be met by simply being born on U.S. soil.

> "The history of the drafting of the Fourteenth Amendment makes clear that the language "subject to the jurisdiction thereof" meant a citizen could not owe allegiance to any other foreign power. This excludes illegal immigrants who are in defiance of U.S. jurisdiction and are citizens of a foreign power.

This section also granted previous slaves citizenship in the States in which they lived and protection and equal treatment under the laws of the States.

Fourteenth Amendment, Section 2

Section 2. Representatives shall be apportioned among the several States according to their respective numbers, counting the whole number of

persons in each State, excluding Indians not taxed. But when the right to vote at any election for the choice of electors for President and Vice President of the United States, Representatives in Congress, the Executive and Judicial officers of a State, or the members of the Legislature thereof, is denied to any of the male inhabitants of such State, being twenty-one years of age, and citizens of the United States, or in any way abridged, except for participation in rebellion, or other crime, the basis of representation therein shall be reduced in the proportion which the number of such male citizens shall bear to the whole number of male citizens twenty-one years of age in such State.

This amendment is the first of five amendments to establish the right to vote. The right to vote is the twenty-seventh separate right listed in the amendments.

This section also removed the references to free persons and the three fifths counting system. It was meant to delete references and any demeaning status to previous slaves.

It is also interesting that all of the discussions of this section never consider the removal of the phrase "and direct taxes" from Article I, Section 2, Paragraph 3. This was a crucial item in the march toward levying direct taxes on the citizens of the United States and it is ignored completely. The removal of this phrase was necessary to begin the implementation of the direct income tax on the people which finally came to fruition with the Sixteenth Amendment. The removal of that phrase also makes this section of the amendment null and void.

Fourteenth Amendment, Section 3

Section 3. No person shall be a Senator or Representative in Congress, or elector of President and Vice President, or hold any office, civil or military, under the United States, or under any State, who, having previously taken an oath, as a member of Congress, or as an officer of the United States, or as a member of any State Legislature, or as an executive or judicial officer of any State, to support the Constitution of the United States, shall have engaged in insurrection or rebellion against the same, or given aid or comfort to the enemies thereof. But Congress may by a vote of two-thirds of each House, remove such disability.

There was a controversy between President Andrew Johnson and the Congress on how to treat previous officials of the Confederacy. President Johnson wanted to be more lenient and Congress wanted to be more strict. This information was obtained from the website Shmoop.com, which is a digital publishing company that seeks to empower and broaden the educational choices that students have available. It is best to be careful and avoid changes that were made by the supreme court when using it.

"Section 3 made it impossible for the president to allow the former leaders of the Confederacy to regain power within the US government after regaining full citizenship rights via blanket presidential pardon; instead, the amendment required a vote of a two thirds majority of Congress itself to allow former Confederate leaders to regain the rights of American citizenship. Unless and until they received that two thirds vote, former Confederate leaders were barred from voting in federal elections or holding federal office.

Fourteenth Amendment, Section 4

Section 4. The validity of the public debt of the United States, authorized by law, including debts incurred for payment of pensions and bounties for services in suppressing insurrection or rebellion, shall not be questioned. But neither the United States nor any State shall assume or pay any debt or obligation incurred in aid of insurrection or rebellion against the United States, or any claim for the loss or emancipation of any slave; but all such

debts, obligations and claims shall be held illegal and void.

Now we come to the debts based on the war. The United States did not want to pay any of the debts caused by the war on personal property, especially that property in the Southern States. This section achieved that purpose. Again comments from Shmoop.com:

"Section 4 prohibited payment of any debt owed to the defunct Confederate States of America and also banned any payment to former slaveholders as compensation for the loss of their human property.

Hundreds of plantations were destroyed. This section, even though not expressly mentioned, also prohibited reimbursement for those plantations.

Fourteenth Amendment, Section 5

Section 5. The Congress shall have power to enforce by appropriate legislation, the provisions of this article

This section gave Congress the power to enforce this amendment.

The Fourteenth Amendment was ratified July 9, 1868.

Fifteenth Amendment

Fifteenth Amendment, Section 1

> **Section 1. The right of citizens of the United States to vote shall not be denied or abridged by the United States or by any State on account of race, color, or previous condition of servitude.**

This amendment was the final of the three amendments created in the aftermath of the Civil War. It is the Second Amendment with the right to vote. In this instance the right of blacks to vote was established.

Actually, this amendment is very clear. Every citizen has the right to vote in federal elections. This amendment was ratified in 1870, and immediately the South set about to make it very difficult for blacks to vote. Special requirements were established that most blacks could not meet.

Today some States are violating this amendment by allowing illegal aliens to have driver's licenses and accepting those licenses as documents entitling them to vote in local, state and federal elections. This is unconstitutional and thus completely illegal. At the same time these States are claiming there is no voter fraud. What hypocrisy!

Fifteenth Amendment, Section 2

Section 2. The Congress shall have power to enforce this article by appropriate legislation.

This section gave Congress the power to enforce this amendment.

The Fifteenth Amendment was ratified February 3, 1870.

Sixteenth Amendment

The Congress shall have power to lay and collect taxes on incomes, from whatever source derived, without apportionment among the several States, and without regard to any census or enumeration.

This is the worst amendment ever. Look closely at the words "without apportionment among the several States, and without regard to any census or enumeration." These words eliminate portions of the Constitution and make the amendment null and void. Now remember the phrase "involuntary servitude" in the Thirteenth Amendment? The Sixteenth Amendment places "involuntary servitude" on every working person in the country in direct violation of Article I, Section 9, Paragraph 4; and Article I, Section 2, Paragraph 3; as they were originally written. This amendment directly taxes all citizens of the United States and causes a portion of their labor to be treated as involuntary servitude. In essence this amendment removes their right to the freedom of their labor. This amendment destroys the fabric of the Declaration of Independence and the intent of the Constitution.

This would be the actual amendment if it were written as it is applied today.

The Congress shall have power to lay and collect taxes on incomes, from whatever source derived, no matter what the Constitution of the United States says.

Then in 1916 the supreme court actually said that this amendment is constitutional in the decision of Brushaber v Union Pacific Railroad Co.

These changes make this amendment legally null and void, per Black's Law Dictionary, but no government official has ever really looked into that. The supreme court is completely out in left field.

Article I, Section 2, Paragraph 3 of the Constitution states:

"direct taxes shall be apportioned among the several States."

And then further on in the same paragraph it states:

"according to their respective Numbers."

Then further on in the same paragraph it states:

"The actual Enumeration shall be made within three years after the first Meeting of the Congress of the United States, and within

216

every subsequent Term of ten Years, in such Manner as they shall by Law Direct.

Then in Article I, Section 9, Paragraph 4, it further states:

"No Capitation, or other direct, Tax shall be laid, unless in Proportion to the Census or Enumeration herein before directed to be taken.

Right! There the rules on taxes are spelled out and are really very clear.

- First – Direct taxes are placed on the States based on their population.
- Second - Congress has powers to collect Duties, Imposts, and Excises. These are taxes on the importation of goods. Article I, Section 8, Paragraph 1.
- Third - Congress has power to levy taxes.
- Fourth - Taxes are laid in proportion to the population of the State.
- Fifth – Taxes will be in proportion to the census taken every ten years.

Income taxes are unconstitutional no matter what the supreme court decides!

The Sixteenth Amendment directly taxes the people and places them in virtual financial slavery in direct violation of all of the goals of the Founding Fathers, In addition, all of the precedents of the supreme court throughout the entire century of the 1800s denied direct taxes on the people. The only purpose of this amendment was to tax the people so they would pay the interest on the massive debt that was to be created by the unconstitutional agency called the Federal Reserve. Today we are paying over $500 billion in interest every year to the owners of the Federal Reserve. The final owners of that organization are the individuals who control the International Banking Establishment. These are the European financiers who are controlling our government with the money we pay them with these illegal interest payments.

The Sixteenth Amendment was ratified February 3, 1913.

Seventeenth Amendment

Seventeenth Amendment, Paragraph 1

> **The Senate of the United States shall be composed of two Senators from each State, elected by the people thereof, for six years; and each Senator shall have one vote. The electors in each State shall have the qualifications requisite for electors of the most numerous branch of the State legislatures.**

This is a change to the wording of the original Constitution and therefore in accordance with Black's Law Dictionary, it is invalid.

This is the second worst amendment ever. The government now basically has two Houses of Representatives which the people control and the States have nothing except the Tenth Amendment which the federal government continually attempts to override.

This amendment destroyed the delicate balance of power of the nation. The Constitution established a balance of power between the people and the States and between the people's representatives and the State's representatives. Remember the States were governments in their own right. They were entities with powers of their own. They gave a portion of their authority to the federal government under certain stipulations. One of those stipulations was a voice in the government itself. That voice was the Senators who represented them, and each State had two Senators who were appointed and expected to look after the interests of the States.

In addition, if you read the last few lines of Article V you will see this:

"and that no State, without its Consent, shall be deprived of its equal Suffrage in the Senate

In other words, the States cannot lose their voting power in the Senate without their permission. This Article of the Constitution prohibited the Seventeenth Amendment before it was even started.

Furthermore, the individuals who began this amendment knew full well what they were doing, and they knew that the people of the United States did not realize what was actually happening. The people just went along with the newspaper stories and editorials and followed like sheep.

Originally, the House of Representatives was to look after the interests of the people, and the Senate was to look after the interests of the States. So, what happened after the Seventeenth Amendment was ratified?

The first and foremost change was to strip the States of their representation in the federal government. That is similar to stripping the people of their representatives in Congress. The International Banking Establishment would have considered this absolutely essential. It allowed them to control the Senators through the people, which is easier than trying to control the State governments. State governments would not be swayed by media sound bites, whereas the people are easily swayed by them. To sway the people the only requirement would be money to pay off the newspapers, and money would be very easy to obtain now that they had their central bank called The Federal Reserve with the ability to keep that money flowing into their coffers.

Another factor that was introduced by the change in the election of the Senators was the ability to create unlimited debt. That has been accomplished par excellence, nearly $22,122,000,000,000 (trillion) and counting.

This is how creating debt was accomplished after taking away the State's representation in the Senate:

First, here are two sections of the Constitution.

Article I, Section 9, Paragraph 4:

"No Capitation, or other direct, Tax shall be laid, unless in Proportion to the Census or Enumeration herein before directed to be taken.

Article I, Section 2, Paragraph 3:

"Representatives and direct Taxes shall be apportioned among the several States which may be included within this Union, according to their respective Numbers, which shall be determined by adding to the whole Number of free Persons, including those bound to Service for a Term of Years, and excluding Indians not taxed, three fifths of all other Persons.

Note the original language in the Constitution concerning direct taxes was changed by the Fourteenth Amendment by removing the three words "and direct taxes." This set the stage for allowing direct taxes on the people. After the change by the Fourteenth Amendment it was easier to get the Sixteenth Amendment through the supreme court.

To begin this analysis it is important to understand that originally the government was funded by import taxes, other levies on imported goods, and lastly from direct taxes on the States. If there was a shortfall, the States were to make it up through direct taxes in proportion to their populations, in accordance with the original language of the above two paragraphs from the Constitution. This was a very simple procedure which kept the government funds mostly in balance. Debts really did not grow exponentially except in emergency situations, like war for instance.

Here is the kicker. The States were required to make up any shortfall and the Senators were the State's representatives. If they passed spending bills that required more money, then the States, who were their bosses, would be very displeased and they could lose their positions. Since they did not want to lose these positions, they closely reviewed spending bills to ensure that overspending did not happen.

The Representatives had to pay attention to the people to get elected. So, to get elected they promised the people all the things that they wanted. When spending bills were introduced, remember the House creates the spending bills, the representatives requested all of the stuff that they had promised the people so they could get reelected.

223

When the bills got to the Senate they looked at the cost and said "no." To protect the States from excessive taxation they required that the spending bills be trimmed down. When the people didn't get what they wanted, the Representatives blamed the Senators. Since the Senators were chosen by the State, they didn't care that the people didn't get what they wanted. They cared that the States were protected. And we must note that most of the items that the people wanted the government to fund were not allowed by the Constitution anyway.

The net effect was that spending was kept under control by and large before the Seventeenth Amendment. Now the people also controlled the Senate so, to get reelected the Senators also began to promise the people what they wanted, and now there was no one looking after the spending, and mountains of money were spent on unconstitutional items.

Then, behind the scenes there was a quiet organization that wanted the Federal Reserve to loan money to the United States to create debt. The Federal Reserve could loan the United States all of the money it wanted, so the federal government could do all of the things that the people wanted. This would result in massive debt and the organization behind the Federal Reserve could collect massive interest. How will this interest be paid? It will be paid by the people. And the payment of the interest by the people was accomplished because the Sixteenth Amendment would insure direct taxes were levied on the people. The part in the Constitution about the States having to pay the shortfall was conveniently ignored, as are all parts of the Constitution that cause difficulties for the political powers.

Who pulled the wool over our eyes as American citizens and taxpayers so that these items would be passed? Why the political parties of course, just like they had been doing ever since 1790 when they began to stop the proper number of Representatives of the people. The political parties are at the bottom of all of these changes, and they got more and more power because of the changes, and power is what they wanted.

All of this occurred because of the power of the International Banking Establishment. The International Banking Establishment is the power behind the throne that has been pulling the strings for centuries.

Seventeenth Amendment, Paragraph 2

When vacancies happen in the representation of any State in the Senate, the executive authority of such State shall issue writs of election to fill such vacancies: Provided, That the legislature of any State may empower the executive thereof to make temporary appointments until the people fill the vacancies by election as the legislature may direct.

This paragraph was written to fill vacancies in the Senate and keep the control of the Senate in the hands of the people and not the State.

Seventeenth Amendment, Paragraph 3

This amendment shall not be so construed as to affect the election or term of any Senator chosen before it becomes valid as part of the Constitution.

This paragraph ensured that the Senators that had already been appointed by the States were not removed.

The Seventeenth Amendment was ratified April 8, 1913.

Eighteenth Amendment

Eighteenth Amendment, Section 1

> **Section 1. After one year from the ratification of this article the manufacture, sale, or transportation of intoxicating liquors within, the importation thereof into, or the exportation thereof from the United States and all territory subject to the jurisdiction thereof for beverage purposes is hereby prohibited.**

This amendment made the manufacture, sale, or transportation of intoxicating liquors illegal. There were good intentions as this amendment was passed but the reality was that black markets became so common that enforcement was literally impossible. It was ratified in 1919 and then repealed in 1933.

Eighteenth Amendment, Section 2

> **Section 2. The Congress and the several States shall have concurrent power to enforce this article by appropriate legislation.**

This section gave Congress and the States the power to enforce this amendment.

Eighteenth Amendment, Section 3

Section 3. This article shall be inoperative unless it shall have been ratified as an amendment to the Constitution by the legislatures of the several States, as provided in the Constitution, within seven years from the date of the submission hereof to the States by the Congress.

Section 3 establishes a time period for ratification. The concept of a time period was not included in the original Constitution and is still a problem; but should be a vital part of the amendment process. There are some who claim that even after 40 years have passed any legislative constitutional convention request is still valid while at the same time these people won't allow any State to revoke a previous approval. New approvals are allowed just no revocations. Those creating these rules will be the individuals who want to destroy the Constitution itself through a new Constitutional Convention and are using Article V as the basis for these actions.

The Eighteenth Amendment was ratified January 16, 1919. It was repealed by the Twenty-First Amendment December 5, 1933.

Nineteenth Amendment

Nineteenth Amendment, Paragraph 1

The right of citizens of the United States to vote shall not be denied or abridged by the United States or by any State on account of sex.

This amendment is the third amendment to include the right to vote. This allowed women to vote in all federal and state elections.

Nineteenth Amendment, Paragraph 2

Congress shall have power to enforce this article by appropriate legislation.

This paragraph gave Congress the power to enforce this amendment.

The Nineteenth Amendment was ratified August 18, 1920.

Twentieth Amendment

Twentieth Amendment, Section 1

> **Section 1. The terms of the President and Vice President shall end at noon on the 20th day of January, and the terms of Senators and Representatives at noon on the 3d day of January, of the years in which such terms would have ended if this article had not been ratified; and the terms of their successors shall then begin.**

The date of the swearing in for the Senators and Representatives was established with this amendment. Originally Washington was sworn in on April 30, 1789. Later the date of inauguration was changed to March 4th based on the day of the year on which the federal government began operations under the U.S. Constitution in 1789. But there was still no official date for the swearing in ceremony. This amendment established that date.

The section also establishes when the successors of the Senators and Representatives shall begin their terms. Section 2 officially establishes the January 3rd date.

Twentieth Amendment, Section 2

Section 2. The Congress shall assemble at least once in every year, and such meeting shall begin at noon on the 3d day of January, unless they shall by law appoint a different day.

Article I, Section 4, Paragraph 2 states:

The Congress shall assemble at least once in every Year, and such Meeting shall be on the first Monday in December, unless they shall by Law appoint a different Day.

The Constitution itself allows for this change. It was difficult to have the Congress convene on the first Monday in December for the next years session. It was reasonable to convene on the first Monday of the next year. But that did create a two month period where the outgoing administration could pass laws during a lame duck period. A lame duck period is the time from election to swearing in. Sometimes this has been very detrimental to the country.

Twentieth Amendment, Section 3

Section 3. If, at the time fixed for the beginning of the term of the President, the President elect shall have died, the Vice President elect shall become President. If a President shall not have been chosen before the time fixed for the beginning of his term, or if the President elect shall have failed to qualify, then the Vice President elect shall act as President until a President shall have qualified; and the Congress may by law provide for the case wherein neither a President elect nor a Vice President elect shall have qualified, declaring who shall then act as President, or the manner in which one who is to act shall be selected, and such person shall act accordingly until a President or Vice President shall have qualified.

Here we have the details controlling how the office of the President and Vice President shall be appointed if the President elect dies or is not qualified. It also clears up the case if the Vice President who would take office for the president elect is not qualified.

Twentieth Amendment, Section 4

Section 4. The Congress may by law provide for the case of the death of any of the persons from whom the House of Representatives may choose a President whenever the right of choice shall have devolved upon them, and for the case of the death of any of the persons from whom the Senate may choose a Vice President whenever the right of choice shall have devolved upon them.

Article II, Section 1, Paragraph 3 provides the rules whereby the president and the vice president will be selected. This section provides for the possibility that one of the possible candidate dies.

Twentieth Amendment, Section 5

Section 5. Sections 1 and 2 shall take effect on the 15th day of October following the ratification of this article.

Here the date is established for this amendment to take effect.

Twentieth Amendment, Section 6

Section 6. This article shall be inoperative unless it shall have been ratified as an amendment to the Constitution by the legislatures of three-fourths of the several States within seven years from the date of its submission.

Section 6 establishes a deadline and the three fourths requirement for ratification.

The Twentieth Amendment was ratified January 23, 1933.

Twenty-First Amendment

Twenty-First Amendment, Section 1

Section 1. The eighteenth article of amendment to the Constitution of the United States is hereby repealed.

This paragraph is very clear. The Eighteenth Amendment is repealed. Intoxicating liquors are now legal again.

This amendment repealed a previous amendment to the Constitution. If one amendment can be repealed why not others? Instead of trying to get a new amendment to do away with the income tax we could do an amendment to repeal the Sixteenth Amendment since it is unconstitutional and shouldn't be enforced anyway.

Twenty-First Amendment, Section 2

Section 2. The transportation or importation into any State, Territory, or possession of the United States for delivery or use therein of intoxicating liquors, in violation of the laws thereof, is hereby prohibited.

This paragraph allows localities to have laws that prohibit the use of intoxicating liquors. States can make their own laws regulating intoxicating liquors and many have.

Twenty-First Amendment, Section 3

Section 3. This article shall be inoperative unless it shall have been ratified as an amendment to the Constitution by conventions in the several States, as provided in the Constitution, within seven years from the date of the submission hereof to the States by the Congress.

Section 3 establishes a time period for ratification

The Twenty-First Amendment was ratified December 5, 1933.

Twenty-Second Amendment

Twenty-Second Amendment, Section 1

> **Section 1. No person shall be elected to the office of the President more than twice, and no person who has held the office of President, or acted as President, for more than two years of a term to which some other person was elected President shall be elected to the office of the President more than once. But this article shall not apply to any person holding the office of President when this Article was proposed by the Congress, and shall not prevent any person who may be holding the office of President, or acting as President, during the term within which this Article becomes operative from holding the office of President or acting as President during the remainder of such term.**

George Washington set a precedence of two terms for the president. That precedence was followed until Franklin D. Roosevelt and he over stepped the bounds to such a degree that this amendment was almost required. It also establishes the details of how the amendment will be treated after ratification.

Twenty-Second Amendment, Section 2

Section 2. This article shall be inoperative unless it shall have been ratified as an amendment to the Constitution by the legislatures of three-fourths of the several States within seven years from the date of its submission to the States by the Congress.

Section 2 establishes a time period and the three fourths requirement for ratification.

The Twenty-Second Amendment was ratified February 27, 1951.

Twenty-Third Amendment

Twenty-Third Amendment, Section 1

Section 1. The District constituting the seat of Government of the United States shall appoint in such manner as the Congress may direct:

A number of electors of President and Vice President equal to the whole number of Senators and Representatives in Congress to which the District would be entitled if it were a State, but in no event more than the least populous State; they shall be in addition to those appointed by the States, but they shall be considered, for the purposes of the election of President and Vice President, to be electors appointed by a State; and they shall meet in the District and perform such duties as provided by the twelfth article of amendment.

This amendment provides the rights of a State to the city called Washington, D.C. Comments from Shmoop.com:

"Washington, D.C. is not a state. The Electoral College, as designed in 1787, grants votes only to states. Therefore, until 1961, people who lived in the District of Columbia weren't able to vote for president. The Twenty-third Amendment gave D.C.

residents a number of presidential electors (3) equal to those of the least populous state.

This is from the Annenberg Classroom:

"In 1800, the District of Columbia became the official seat of government. When first established, the town had a small population of only five thousand residents. As a federal territory, however, and not a state, the inhabitants had neither a local government, nor the right to vote in federal elections. Although by 1960 the population of the District of Columbia had grown to over 760,000 people, and District residents had all the responsibilities of citizenship— they were required to pay federal taxes and could be drafted to serve in the military— citizens in thirteen states with lower populations had more voting rights than District residents.

It might appear that this is an appropriate change to the Constitution, but it does change the wording of the Constitution, which is the contract between the people and the States and the federal government. Therefore, this change of the contract is null and void according to Black's Law Dictionary.

Twenty-Third Amendment, Section 2

Section 2. The Congress shall have power to enforce this article by appropriate legislation.

This section gave Congress the power to enforce this amendment.

The Twenty-Third Amendment was ratified March 29, 1961.

Twenty-Fourth Amendment

Twenty-Fourth Amendment, Section 1

> **Section 1. The right of citizens of the United States to vote in any primary or other election for President or Vice President, for electors for President or Vice President, or for Senator or Representative in Congress, shall not be denied or abridged by the United States or any State by reason of failure to pay any poll tax or other tax.**

This is the fourth instance giving citizens the right to vote. In this instance the poll tax was outlawed for any federal elected office. Poll taxes were another method to prevent the black race from voting.

Twenty-Fourth Amendment, Section 2

> **Section 2. The Congress shall have power to enforce this article by appropriate legislation.**

This section gave Congress the power to enforce this amendment.

The Twenty-Fourth Amendment was ratified January 23, 1964

Twenty-Fifth Amendment

In Article II, Section 1, Paragraph 6, many questions can arise, not the least of which is who shall decide that the President is not fit for duty? This lengthy amendment does not really answer that question. As we discuss this amendment we will see that most of the problems inherent in the actual Constitution are not really improved upon. As mentioned previously in volume three of *The Founders' Constitution* the problems are not really discussed either. Let's review this amendment and see what has happened. Another major problem is that this amendment changes the wording of the Constitution, or the contract, and that makes it null and void according to Black's Law Dictionary.

Twenty-Fifth Amendment, Section 1

> **Section 1. In case of the removal of the President from office or of his death or resignation, the Vice President shall become President.**

Here are some comments about Article II, Section 1, Paragraph 6, from Justia.com concerning Presidential Succession. Justia.com is a website which provides free case law, codes, regulations and legal information for lawyers, businesses, students and consumers world wide.

"When the President is disabled or is removed or has died, to what does the Vice President succeed: to the "powers and duties of the said office," or to the office itself? There is a reasonable amount of evidence from the proceedings of the Convention from which to conclude that the Framers intended the Vice President to remain Vice President and to exercise the powers of the President until, in the words of the final clause, "a President shall be elected." Nonetheless, when President Harrison died in 1841, Vice President Tyler, after initial hesitation, took the position that he was automatically President, a precedent which has been followed subsequently and which is now permanently settled by section 1 of the Twenty-fifth Amendment. That Amendment also settles a number of other pressing questions with regard to presidential inability and succession.

This portion of the amendment does correct the problems mentioned in the quote above, but the word removal is still not discussed.

There are changes to the wording of the Constitution in this amendment, concerning the duties of the Vice President and therefore the amendment is unconstitutional. But even though it is probably apparent that the wording of the Constitution is not as clear as it should be and needs clarification this was not the proper procedure.

This amendment was ratified in 1967 and this was during a time when some were calling for a new constitutional convention and that could have been disastrous. But if a change needed to be made this was the only way to do it.

I would have left section 1 out and then the amendment would be legal.

Twenty-Fifth Amendment, Section 2

Section 2. Whenever there is a vacancy in the office of the Vice President, the President shall nominate a Vice President who shall take office upon confirmation by a majority vote of both Houses of Congress.

This section allows the President to appoint a Vice President if necessary and since this section changes the mode of electing the President it is also legally null and void.

Twenty-Fifth Amendment, Section 3

Section 3. Whenever the President transmits to the President pro tempore of the Senate and the Speaker of the House of Representatives his written declaration that he is unable to discharge the powers and duties of his office, and until he transmits to them a written declaration to the contrary, such powers and duties shall be discharged by the Vice President as Acting President.

This section sets a procedure for the president to admit that he is unable to function. Then the procedure is also included that when he is again able to function he can transmit another letter allowing him to assume the duties without approval of the Congress.

Twenty-Fifth Amendment, Section 4, Paragraph 1

Section 4. Whenever the Vice President and a majority of either the principle officers of the executive departments or of such other body as Congress may by law provide, transmit to the President pro tempore of the Senate and the Speaker of the House of Representatives their written declaration that the President is unable to discharge the powers and duties of his office, the Vice President shall immediately assume the powers and duties of the office as Acting President.

This section creates a significant problem. It specifies that a selected group of individuals have the authority to remove the president whenever it suits them. In the political situation we currently have, Congress could select a body of individuals that would have the authority to remove President Trump. This designated group could be composed of individuals who just want him out of there. There is a movie that shows this procedure in operation and only because the Vice-President doesn't sign the document the president still remained in office. This section provides for an environment in which a dictatorship could be created.

Twenty-Fifth Amendment, Section 4, Paragraph 2

> **Thereafter, when the President transmits to the President pro tempore of the Senate and the Speaker of the House of Representatives his written declaration that no inability exists, he shall resume the powers and duties of his office unless the Vice President and a majority of either the principal officers of the executive department or of such other body as Congress may by law provide, transmit within four days to the President pro tempore of the Senate and the Speaker of the House of Representatives their written declaration that the President is unable to discharge the**

powers and duties of his office. Thereupon Congress shall decide the issue, assembling within forty-eight hours for that purpose if not in session. If the Congress, within twenty-one days after receipt of the latter written declaration, or, if Congress is not in session, within twenty-one days after Congress is required to assemble, determines by two-thirds vote of both Houses that the President is unable to discharge the powers and duties of his office, the Vice President shall continue to discharge the same as Acting President; otherwise, the President shall resume the powers and duties of his office.

This is a very lengthy paragraph and quite difficult to understand but in essence it provides for the same people as listed in the previous paragraph the power to override the president's letter. Details including the number of days to take action are mentioned, but the power still resides in those few people to determine the inability of the president to perform.

Now, the definition of what constitutes inability to perform the office, comes into full swing. What does that mean? If these people are just out to get him because they don't like his policies are they justified in their actions? This kind of wording could become the basis for another civil war or rebellion.

250

The word "removal" is the key problem of this amendment and of the Constitution itself. That word needs to be resolved before someone tries to remove the President just based on personality differences. The amendment has been ratified and has left us in a dangerous position.

The Twenty-Fifth Amendment was ratified February 10, 1967.

Twenty-Sixth Amendment

Twenty-Sixth Amendment, Section 1

> **Section 1. The right of citizens of the United States, who are eighteen years of age or older, to vote shall not be denied or abridged by the United States or by any State on account of age.**

This is the fifth instance establishing the right to vote. In this case the age of voting was reduced from 21 to 18. The basis of this age change was to allow individuals who were required to fight in the military forces the right to vote. It allowed combatants who were putting their lives and well being on the line the right to vote for the federal officials who were requiring them to fight.

Since the Constitution doesn't address the date a person becomes eligible to vote this is a valid change and is a proper amendment.

Twenty-Sixth Amendment, Section 2

> **Section 2. The Congress shall have power to enforce this article by appropriate legislation.**

This section gave Congress the power to enforce this amendment.

The Twenty-Sixth Amendment was Ratified July 1, 1971.

Twenty-Seventh Amendment

No law, varying the compensation for the services of the Senators and Representatives, shall take effect, until an election of Representatives shall have intervened.

These comments are from Shmoop.com:

"The Twenty-seventh Amendment bars members of Congress from voting to give themselves a pay raise. They may vote to raise congressional pay, but such increases can take effect only after the next election.

"The most interesting thing about the Twenty-seventh Amendment, by far, is its history. The Twenty-seventh Amendment was one of the original package of twelve passed by the First Congress in 1789. Ten of those twelve gained ratification in 1791; we have known them ever since as the Bill of Rights, the famous Amendments 1 to 10 of the Constitution. But this amendment waited in limbo for more than 200 years before finally gaining ratification from three fourths of the states and becoming law. That is a record that surely will never be broken!

Congress submitted the text of the Twenty-Seventh Amendment to the States as part of the proposed Bill of Rights on September 25, 1789. The Amendment was not ratified together with the first ten Amendments, which became effective on December 15, 1791. The Twenty-Seventh Amendment was ratified on May 7, 1992, by the vote of Michigan.

Conclusion

This book was written to explain the wording of the original Constitution. Books written about the Constitution usually take the precedences that the supreme court has written during the last 225 years and teach them as the Constitution. The supreme court has no authority to change the Constitution! We should concentrate on what the actual original Constitution says. Decisions similar to the case of Marbury v Madison in 1803 and the case of Ware v Hylton in 1796 have completely changed the meaning of the Constitution. As a nation we must return to the actual Constitution as envisioned by the Founding Fathers in 1787.

There are undoubtedly mistakes in this work, and I would appreciate and will review any that are pointed out to me. Please do not use supreme court decisions or illegal amendments as the source for any comments. Usually these are cases where prejudices and individual agendas have been used as the basis for changing the Constitution. These changes are illegal and should be nullified and ignored. Nobody has the authority to change the words or punctuation of the Constitution.

My intent has been to show what was originally written and what the Founders intended for the document to mean. Seven of the amendments that have been added since 1788 actually completely change the meaning of the Constitution because they change the actual wording. If an amendment changes the words of a contract, the amendment is null and void. The Sixteenth and Seventeenth Amendments are accurate representations of changing and ignoring the words of the Constitution and demonstrate the accuracy of the above sentence.

If we understood what the Constitution actually meant and still means and then returned our governments, both state and federal, to the intentions of the Founding Fathers, many of the current problems of our nation would completely disappear. This book was written to bring the discrepancies that have occurred over time to the reader's attention.

Now what can the states do today to begin correcting the errors that have occurred? Remember the states are sovereign entities. nations in their own right. To easily understand what should be done, I will present the ideas in steps. These steps are actually included throughout this book but are obscure, so I have listed them in order here. None of these steps can be accomplished until the state legislative bodies are more constitutionally minded.

- First - We must realize that all state legislators, governors, and judges have taken an oath to support the Constitution against all enemies foreign or domestic. This requirement is found in Article VI Paragraph 3. This oath constitutes a responsibility to adhere to the principles of the Constitution. This means that every law, decision, rule, or program that is decreed by the federal government that is not a part of the original Constitution is illegal and must be nullified in each state. There will be growing pains, but remember the goal. This step is a part of contract law found in Black's Law Dictionary.
- Second - The states must simultaneously authorize a militia and a public citizens bank. The Second Amendment specifies "A well regulated Militia, being

necessary to the security of a free State." When the Constitution uses the word State it is referring to the states of that time: Virginia, New York, Massachusetts, etc. Today's equivalent includes those states and all of the new ones such as Iowa, Kansas, Montana, etc. Each state needs this militia to secure their viability as a sovereign and independent state. The public citizens bank is completely described in Volume 6 of my Liberty series, but it is basically the means to finance the operations of the state without money from the federal government.

- Third – The state must nullify the Seventeenth Amendment. It is completely unconstitutional per Article I and Article V. The last few words of Article V are " no State, without its Consent, shall be deprived of its equal Suffrage in the Senate." That very clearly says that they cannot lose their representation in the Senate. The state must nullify the popular election of the Senators and appoint new Senators as each state feels is necessary to follow the Constitution   Then the state must review the voting records of their current two Senators, and if that record indicates that either Senator has violated the Constitution, that Senator should be replaced immediately and another appointed in his place.

- Fourth – The state must provide for the proper number of Representatives. Per Article I, Section 2, Paragraph 3, a representative cannot represent more than thirty thousand citizens.   The state must establish new precincts to provide for the election by the people of the proper number of representatives. Some might say that the House of Representatives will not seat those individuals. There is no provision for the House to deny those properly elected representatives a place in the House. The House may have established some rules or laws concerning the number of Representatives each state can have; but those rules or laws cannot be considered superior to the Constitution itself per Article VI, Paragraph 2.

- Fifth – The state must nullify the Sixteenth Amendment, as it is completely unconstitutional! The federal government might attempt to prosecute any individual taxpayer who refuses to submit a form 1040, but those individuals can point to the laws of the state that they must follow. The federal government may attempt to coerce the state into continuing to follow unconstitutional laws or decisions by cutting off all funding that the state might receive from the federal government. Since a public citizens bank has been formed and its operations will provide sufficient funds to operate the state, there will be no need for any federal funds.

In addition to the above there are many more laws to nullify, and that is part of the reason for the militia. There must be some force belonging to the state that can ensure that the state laws in accordance with the Constitution are not set aside by the federal government. Federal marshals will be sent, and the militia will politely escort them to the border.

It will be very difficult to follow these suggestions, as it is not easy to change anything that has been in operation for so many years. The Revolutionary War was not easy either, but it was necessary to obtain our liberties. Those liberties are the final goal. We must return our nation to what was envisioned by the Founding Fathers. as they wrote and signed the Declaration of Independence and the Constitution.

Appendix 1

Admiralty and Maritime Jurisdiction

In Article III, Section 2, Paragraph 1, the federal courts are authorized to see cases of admiralty and maritime jurisdiction. These are cases involving the high seas and not cases that are internal within one of the States of the convention of 1787. The Founders understood this distinction, which has been lost over time. The following from Wikipedia:

> Admiralty law or maritime law is a body of law that governs nautical issues and private maritime disputes. Admiralty law consists of both domestic law on maritime activities, and private international law governing the relationships between private parties operating or using ocean-going ships. While each legal jurisdiction usually has its own legislation governing maritime matters, the international nature of the topic and the need for uniformity has, since 1900, led to considerable international maritime law developments, including numerous multilateral treaties.

Currently, our courts have evolved to the point that they pass judgments on cases that are actually maritime cases. Since we are ignorant of these discrepancies, the court gets away with treating these cases as criminal or civil cases.

Victimless cases are another area. What is the definition of victimless? It is having no victim: not of a nature that may produce a complainant is a victimless crime

A major feature of Admiralty Law is the victimless crime. The captain of the ship has full authority to punish even if there is no loss of any kind. The premise is that if the order is disobeyed significant loss is probable. That premise does not exist on land. If a person is speeding, there is no presumption that injury or loss would occur. An obvious example is that speeding is a natural event on the roads of America without any loss or injury. However if a seaman refuses to obey orders, the ship could and often would sustain serious damage including loss of life.

The premise could be: If there is no victim there is no crime. In order for a court to punish a victimless case, which are not just traffic cases, there must be an actual claim of injury. No injury, no jurisdiction, no legal authority, it's that simple. These victimless cases are often really maritime jurisdiction cases. They are not criminal or civil law cases and should not be in our normal court system.

Since victimless cases are not criminal cases, we must know how to treat noncriminal cases. What did the Founders say? The documents available in *The Founders' Constitution* in Volume 5 on pages 343-367 show that adding trial by jury to civil cases was a major issue. Some of the colonies tried civil cases by jury and others did not. All of them seemed to differ in how the civil cases would be handled. Jury trials could be a hardship on the jurors as they might have to travel great distances.

Because of these difficulties, there had to be some type of limit on when trial by jury was appropriate. Since losses were really the reason for these cases, a limit was established on the minimum loss that would be required to have a jury trial.

The result of these discussions was that a loss or injury had to be established for the case to come to court, and the jury trial had to have a loss of at least $20. This part of the Constitution secured the rule that an injury was required for a civil case.

There are usually three different types of court cases: criminal, civil, and maritime or maritime jurisdiction. Each of these have different rules. Criminal cases can always have a jury and are against a government law usually considered an evil act like robbery or murder. Civil cases are usually cases that are between two people or groups. They are often differences of opinion that cannot be solved by the individuals. Constitutionally, these cases must have an injury or loss of some kind that exceeds $20 to have a jury trial. Maritime jurisdiction are cases that have to do with violations on the water, or navigable rivers, the bays, or the oceans.

In maritime jurisdiction the captain is the absolute authority. That individual accuses, tries, and punishes at the same time without appeal. This is necessary for the safety of the vessel. It is interesting that we have allowed that same privilege to judges in courts of law. It is called contempt of court and a person can immediately be taken and incarcerated just by the demand of the judge. That seems to be contrary to our common rule of law. It is supposedly justified so that the court has some order, but it is often abused by over zealous judges.

What about those victimless cases that were previously discussed? Remember these are cases where there is no loss or injury. Most of our traffic courts are of this nature. A person accused of speeding is tried and convicted of a possible crime that might have happened because of the excess speed. Even though there has been no actual injury or loss the person is convicted because sometimes a loss occurs because of the excess speed. If that were correct, anyone boiling water on the stove could be convicted of a crime, as boiling water has been known to spill on the cook and cause injury. That seems ridiculous, but it has the same basis as a punishment for speeding. That type of law would be considered a violation of the Fourth Amendment as we are considered secure in our property.

The only way a law of that type can apply is in a maritime court. And even then there are specific requirements of:

> "...personal jurisdiction in the matter of a victimless traffic violation, let's back up and find out exactly what constitutes the gaining of jurisdiction for a court in such a matter.

> "In order for any court to gain jurisdiction in a matter that is brought before it, that court must have established on the record the two elements that constitute jurisdiction. Those two elements are personal jurisdiction and what is known as subject matter jurisdiction. When demanded (and it is always a good idea for the accused to make this demand) these two elements of jurisdiction must appear on the record of the court or the court is operating without any authority. It is the duty of the party bringing the action (the so-called plaintiff) to

264

prove both personal and subject matter jurisdiction before a matter can even be brought to a court. It is not the duty of the court (or the judge) to prove these elements of jurisdiction. Yet, because most people are ignorant of legal process, they do not understand that it is the plaintiff who assumes the burden of proving these elements with hard evidence entered on the record before the matter can proceed forward. A mere unsworn to accusation or complaint is not hard evidence of anything! Only sworn testimony from a competent injured party can stand as a verified complaint in order to provide evidence of jurisdiction.

"While a judge is within his authority to assert that he can hear a certain matter within the parameters of a given subject matter such as a traffic violation, this is not the same as having subject matter jurisdiction proven on the record. There is a maxim of law which states: "What is like is not the same, for nothing similar is the same." In other words, a simple assertion that the court can hear any variety of matters involving traffic violations does not reach the level of a specific matter being brought before the court by a specific injured party. There has to be a specific matter brought before a court before the matter can proceed in that court. If no one has an actual claim of injury or property damage, then subject matter jurisdiction has not been established! It is that simple. From "Common Law Remedy - The Two Faces of Jurisdiction BeatTrafficTickets.org"

Jurisdiction is so important that without it being properly determined there could be no case at all. From Admiralty and Navigable Water Bodies – Not Just Jurisdictional Issues by Stephen Boutwell, December 5, 2016 posted in Admiralty and Maritime:

"As the plaintiff in this case learned, jurisdiction is a pivotally-important element of any case. Not only can it determine which court can hear a plaintiff's case, but in some instances it may also dictate the law applicable to the plaintiff's claims. And, especially in cases of personal injuries occurring on the often shallow waters of South Louisiana, it may determine whether a plaintiff has a case at all.

To be a navigable waterway, the waterway must be used or must be capable of being used in its ordinary condition as a "highway for commerce."

This has been a long and circuitous discussion, but it entails several types of law. It would behoove those who have more interest than this brief discussion to do further research using these comments as a basis.

A last point. It is felt the the gold fringe on the American flag displayed in court, establishes that the court is a maritime court. That is not correct. The gold fringe is a decorative item and can be used by anyone as desired.

Appendix 2

Treaties Don't Override the Constitution

Appendix 2 is an outstanding document written by Don Fotheringham explaining in great detail the third paragraph of Article VI emphasizing the true application of treaties with other nations or organizations.

Beware the False Idea That Treaties Override the Constitution Article VI, Paragraph 3

By Don Fotheringham
Past Member of the Board of Directors of the Freedom First Society
Member of the Academy of Political Science
Author of *The President Makers*

The ridiculous idea that U.S. treaties with foreign nations supersede the Constitution has been around since the Eisenhower era. (See note 1 below.) It came on the scene in 1952 when Secretary of State John Foster Dulles, a founding member of the Council on Foreign Relations (CFR), made the following statement:

"...congressional laws are invalid if they do not conform to the Constitution, whereas treaty laws can override the Constitution. Treaties, for example, can take powers away from Congress and give then to the President; they can take powers from the states and give them to the Federal Government, or to some international body and they can cut across the rights given the people by the Constitutional Bill of Rights. (Dulles actually made this statement shortly before Eisenhower appointed him Secretary of State. Quoted by Frank E. Holman, Story of the Bricker Amendment, pp. 14-15.)

It would be hard to find a more preposterous assertion. Sadly, however, many citizens have been led to believe that treaties do override the Constitution. Could anyone really think that our Founding Fathers spent four months in convention, limiting the size, power and scope of government, and then provided for their work to be destroyed by one lousy treaty? Article VI establishes the supremacy of U.S. laws and treaties made within the bounds of the Constitution.

This was needed because, contrary to their agreement under the Articles of Confederation, certain states violated their trust and entered into treaties with foreign powers. During the convention, Madison said, "Experience had evinced a constant tendency in the States to encroach on the federal authority, to violate national Treaties, to infringe the rights & interests of each other." (Records of the Convention of 1787, Farrand, Vol, I, p. 16.4)

State-made pacts often conflicted with peace and trade treaties wanted by the Confederation Congress. This made it

268

hard for Congress to consummate better agreements with other nations. This also led to contention between the states while some tried to monopolize the import of goods from Europe and the Indian Tribes. But the most serious danger arose in matters of security, for should one state be at war with a foreign power while a sister state honors its peace agreement with that power, the security of the entire Confederation would be at stake. (Benjamin Franklin's Plan of Union, America, Vol. 3, p 47.)

In order to head off such a situation, the Confederation Congress frequently attempted to nullify state-made agreements in the state courts (there were no federal courts). But as might be expected, the state judges ruled inevitability in favor of their own states, pursuant to their state laws and constitutions.

The 1787 Convention corrected that problem by making certain only federal treaties would be recognized as valid and that the state courts could not rule otherwise. In this light, it is not hard to understand why paragraph two of Article VI is worded as follows:

"This Constitution, and the Laws of the United States which shall be made in Pursuance thereof, and all Treaties made, or which shall be made, under the Authority of the United States, shall be the supreme Law of the Land; and the Judges in every State shall be bound thereby, any Thing in the Constitution or Laws of any State to the Contrary notwithstanding.

Upon ratification of the Constitution, all state-made treaties were nullified. Thereafter, only federal treaties were recognized as supreme, regardless of any remaining state

269

provisions to the contrary.   Moreover, under the new Constitution the Founders established a supreme court, granting it original jurisdiction over treaty controversies and thereby removing such cases from the jurisdiction of state judges. In addition to quelling strife among the states, Article VI accomplished a major objective of the Constitution, mainly that of placing the United States in the position of speaking to the world with one voice. (See Note 2 below.)

United States treaties are created when proposed by the President, with the advice and consent of the Senate. The power of the President and the Senate, in their treaty-making capacity, was never intended to be a power that could exceed constitutional limits.

A correct understanding of the Supremacy Clause was gained by citizens who met in the state ratifying conventions (1787 to 1790) where they examined with great care provisions of the proposed Constitution. During the ratifying debates, James Madison answered questions regarding the new national charter, and commented on the extent of the treaty-making power under Article VI:

> "I do not conceive that power is given to the President and Senate to dismember the empire, or to alienate any great, essential right. I do not think the whole legislative authority have this power. The exercise of the power must be consistent with the object of its delegation. (Debates on the Federal Constitution, Jonathan Elliot, ed., 2nd ed. Philadelphia, J.B. Lippincott Company, 1907, Vol. III, p. 514.)

In the same discussion Madison said, "Here, the supremacy of a treaty is contrasted with the supremacy of the laws of the states. It cannot be otherwise supreme." That is, a treaty cannot in any other manner or situation be supreme.

Thomas Jefferson: "I say the same as to the opinion of those who consider the grant of treaty-making to be boundless. If it is, then we have no Constitution."

Note from R. Proctor: As covered previously in this book the first instance of this idea that treaties supersede the Constitution was in 1796 with the supreme court decision in the case Ware v. Hilton. The second instance was in 1920 with the supreme court decision in the case of Missouri v Holland. The third instance was in 1942 with the supreme court decision in the case of United States v Pink. There may also have been other instances of the federal government violating Article VI in this fashion.

Index

A

B

C

279

97, 98, 100, 102, 103, 104, 105, 107, 108, 109, 112, 114, 115, 116, 117, 119, 120, 121, 124, 125, 129, 130, 131, 138, 142, 155, 156, 158, 160, 195, 204, 207, 208, 209, 210, 214, 215, 217, 221, 227, 228, 229, 232, 233, 236, 237, 238, 239, 241, 243, 247, 248, 249, 250, 253, 255, 256, 268, 269

draft - 203, 204, 240
driver's licenses - 213
due process of law - 177, 178, 203, 205
Dulles, John Foster - 267, 368
duties - 20, 50, 51, 76, 79, 92, 94, 95, 97, 101, 217, 239, 246, 247, 248, 249, 250

E

Eastern states - 89
education - 1, 119, 317
educational - 208
educators - 9
eight - 17, 26, 111, 149, 196
eighteen years of age - 253
Eisenhower, Dwight D., President - 158, 267, 268
election - 259
election fraud - 86
Electoral College - 8, 31, 83, 86, 87, 88, 89, 200, 201, 239
electors - 24, 83, 84, 85, 90, 199, 200, 207, 219, 239, 240, 243
Electronic Frontier Foundation (EFF) - 173, 174, 175
emolument - 47, 78, 98, 99
endless list of rights - 151
enemies - 11, 45, 64, 116, 117, 188, 208, 258
engage in war - 80, 81
Engel v Vitale (1962) - 160
England - 28, 188
English Law - 92
enjoyment - 22, 148
enslavement - 62
entities - 17, 19, 145, 178, 194, 219
enumeration - 26, 29, 75, 151, 191, 215, 216, 217, 222

F

285

foreign nations - 10, 51, 53, 61, 62, 80
foreigners - 8, 20
foreign powers - 20, 80, 196, 197, 206, 268, 269
forfeiture - 46, 117, 187
form 1040 - 260
forts - 68
foster evil - 85
Fotheringham, Don - 267
Founders - 9, 21, 22, 37, 41, 55, 73, 75, 78, 85, 90, 93, 101, 133, 135, 156, 165, 166, 188, 189, 257, 261, 270
Founding Fathers - 6, 9, 46, 69, 137, 140, 178, 218, 257, 258, 260, 268
four years - 83
fourteen years - 90
free agency - 13
free persons - 26, 207, 222
free state - 122, 165, 259
freedom - 3, 4, 13, 107, 147, 151, 152, 155, 156, 157, 159, 160, 161, 162, 191, 215
Freedom First Society - 267
Freedom from Government-Over-Man - 151
freedom from poverty - 191
freedom from want - 191
freedom of religion - 4, 159, 160
freedom of speech - 4, 155, 160, 161, 162
freedom of the press - 4, 155, 162
freedom to establish a religion - 155
freedom to exercise your religion - 4, 155
Freedom-Responsibility - 147
fugitive - 121, 122
full faith and credit - 119
funds - 32, 52, 223
Furman v Georgia (1972) - 188

G

gagged - 159
gardens - 53
gender - 161
general Welfare - 19, 20, 21, 50, 51
geographical area - 19, 76
Georgetown University Law Center - 73
Georgia - 27, 144, 188, 195, 187
God - 2, 13, 39, 127, 146, 147, 148, 149, 150, 153, 158, 191
God-given rights - 146, 147, 150
God's Law - 113, 147
gold - 78, 79
gold fringe - 266
gold standard - 317
good behavior - 107, 109
govern - 194
government - 3, 4, 5, 7, 8, 10, 13, 14, 15, 16, 17, 19, 22, 23, 29, 30, 34, 48, 51, 52, 54, 56, 59, 64, 65, 68, 69, 70, 74, 75, 76, 77, 78, 85, 99, 100, 101, 103, 104, 128, 130, 132, 133, 135, 139, 145, 146, 147, 148, 149, 150, 151, 152, 153, 155, 156, 157, 158, 160, 161, 163, 164, 167, 168, 169, 170, 171, 172, 175, 178, 179, 180, 188, 190, 204, 216, 218, 219, 220, 223, 224, 239, 240, 317
government agencies - 69
government employee - 99
governors - 258
grand jury - 5, 177
Great Britain - 137
Great Depreciation - 8
greater tax base - 180
groups of people - 20

H

I

innocent - 172, 173, 174, 177, 182
innumerable rights - 151
inspection laws - 79
insulting - 162
insure domestic Tranquility - 19, 20
insurrections - 66, 208, 209
intent - 37, 119, 129, 163, 177, 215, 257
intention - 1, 20, 52, 168, 227, 258
interest (money) - 52, 56, 70, 165, 170, 218, 225, 317
international - 62, 64, 261, 268
International Banking Establishment - 7, 8, 218, 221, 225
interstate commerce - 10
intoxicating liquors - 227, 235, 236
invading - 20, 80, 81
invasion - 66, 72, 81, 126
inventors - 59
involuntary servitude - 122, 203, 204, 215
Iowa - 166, 259
is not qualified - 233
Italy - 70

J

January - 89, 100, 228, 231, 232, 234, 243, 317
Jefferson, Thomas - 108, 127, 148, 271
jeopardize - 80, 158
Johnson, Andrew, President - 208
Johnson, Lyndon Baines, President - 105, 156, 157, 158
Johnson, William, Justice - 74
journal - 43, 49
journalism - 163
journalists - 162, 163

K

L

licenses - 64, 121, 156, 168, 213
licensing - 168
lie - 89, 106, 163
life or limb - 177
lifetime appointment - 109
limit - 3, 15, 16, 24, 31, 50, 59, 69, 77, 91, 109, 112, 149, 150, 172, 187, 191, 221
Lincoln, Abraham, President - 2, 125
liquor - 227, 235, 236
Living Constitution - 113
loan - 28, 56, 132, 224
loss - 47, 168, 169, 186, 210
Louisiana - 266
low regard - 100
Lucas v South Carolina Coastal Council (1992) - 179

M

Madison, James - 144, 268, 270
magazines - 68
mail - 58, 59, 164
mail coaches - 59
majority - 24, 32, 41, 42, 84, 85, 87, 199, 200, 209, 247, 248, 249
malicious - 163
manipulation - 56
manufacture - 70, 227
Marbury v Madison (1803) - 107, 108, 112, 257
March - 98, 200, 207, 231, 241
March 4th - 231
Marines - 65
maritime - 110, 112, 186, 261, 262, 263, 264, 266
marry - 119

Marshall, John J., Chief Justice - 8, 9, 10, 74, 107, 108, 112
Martin v Hunter - 194
Maryland - 26, 144
Massachusetts - 26, 143, 259
maxim of law - 265
May - 204, 256
media - 47, 162, 182, 220, 221
medium of exchange - 79
Men in Black - 109
mental patient - 72
Merriam-Webster Dictionary - 146
Merry Christmas - 160
Michigan - 127
Middle Ages - 64
migration - 71
military exercises - 66
military force - 65, 66, 253
militia - 65, 66, 67, 101, 165, 166, 167, 177, 194, 258, 259, 260
Miller v Alabama (2012) - 189
minimum wages - 167, 168
ministers - 102, 103, 105, 110, 112, 114, 159
Minnesota - 127
miscellaneous - 119
misfortune - 22
Missouri v Holland (1920) - 138, 271
mode of ratification - 129, 130
monetary value - 99
money - 7, 8, 21, 27, 52, 55, 56, 57, 58, 65, 70, 77, 78, 102, 120, 170, 182, 218, 221, 223, 224
money supply - 8, 56
Monopoly money - 52
Montana - 259
moral - 11, 113, 147, 148, 157, 160

more than twice - 237
most qualified - 86
murder - 263
murdered - 189
mutilation - 188

N

name - 17, 49, 87, 105, 122, 138, 141, 151, 161, 199
nation - 9, 14, 15, 16, 19, 20, 21, 28, 53, 55, 57, 70, 76, 80, 134, 156, 158, 201, 279, 257, 258, 260
national forests - 69
national monuments - 69
national parks - 69
national religion - 156
nativity scenes - 160
natural born citizen - 90, 91
naturalization - 54, 91
nature of the accusation - 5, 181
Nature's Law - 113, 186
nautical - 261
naval forces - 65, 177
navigable - 263, 266
navy - 65, 97, 101
needful buildings - 68
nefarious - 160
net produce - 79
New Hampshire - 26, 143
New Jersey - 26, 119, 143
New Mexico - 121
new states - 16, 124, 127
New York - 26, 138, 143, 163, 166, 259
New York Times Company v Sullivan (1964) - 163

O

offense - 40, 60, 61, 101, 177, 178, 179, 187
Ohio - 127, 166
omitted - 131, 151
once in every year - 41, 232
one-third - 35, 85, 172, 204
One World Order - 50
opinion - 23, 91, 101, 102, 136, 161, 163, 182, 185
order - 4, 19, 21, 23, 50, 53, 93, 97, 119, 120, 121, 153
original jurisdiction - 114
original package of twelve amendments - 255
our own use - 10, 53
own weapons - 66

P

parchment - 1
pardons - 101
parental citizenship - 91
parents - 14
patents - 59
patriotic - 87
pay raise - 255
payment of debts - 79
payoffs - 56
peace - 5, 21, 22, 45, 46, 61, 80, 119, 155, 167, 179, 268,
269
Peace Corps - 203
Pennsylvania - 26, 144
People - 1, 4, 19, 24, 34, 38, 132, 133, 145, 155, 163, 165,
166, 171, 191, 193, 204, 219, 226
people - 1, 6, 7, 10, 13, 14, 15, 16, 19, 20, 21, 23, 24, 27, 29,
30, 31, 32, 34, 35, 38, 48, 51, 54, 57, 72, 75, 78, 86, 87, 88,
89, 100, 106, 108, 115, 121, 126, 132, 140, 148, 149, 150,

post roads - 58, 59
postal mail - 58
posterity - 19, 22, 148
power - 1, 3, 4, 7, 8, 9, 10, 14, 15, 20, 23, 28, 29, 30, 33, 34, 35, 36, 37, 38, 40, 42, 50, 55, 60, 69, 70, 76, 77, 80, 83, 92, 93, 94, 95, 97, 101, 102, 103, 104, 109, 110, 115, 117, 120, 125, 126, 131, 133, 138, 145, 147, 149, 150, 152, 180, 193, 194, 196, 197, 204, 206, 208, 209, 210, 214, 215, 216, 217, 219, 220, 225, 227, 229, 241, 243, 246, 248, 249, 250, 253
power of the purse - 77
power over the military - 101
powers not delegated - 193
prayer - 2, 160
preamble - 17, 19, 20, 21, 22
precedent law - 113
precedents - 2, 67, 113, 114, 131, 218, 246
precincts - 259
presidency - 13, 93
president - 8, 13, 15, 23, 36, 37, 38, 42, 49, 50, 83, 84, 85, 86, 87, 88, 89, 90, 91, 92, 93, 94, 95, 96, 97, 98, 99, 101, 102, 103, 104, 105, 106, 138, 199, 200, 201, 207, 208, 209, 231, 232, 233, 234, 237, 239, 243, 245, 246, 247, 248, 249, 250, 251, 268, 270
president elect dies - 233
President of the Senate - 36, 84, 199
president pro tempore - 37, 94, 95, 199, 248, 249
presidential election - 86
presidential succession - 245
press - 4, 155, 162, 163
presto - 68
prisoner - 62, 72, 121
prisoners of war - 62
private company - 8
private property rights - 167, 168

Q

qualifications - 24, 25, 36, 41, 90, 139, 219
qualify - 86, 94, 95, 96, 97, 136, 137, 168, 174, 233
quartered - 167
Quorum - 41, 42, 44, 84, 199, 200

R

racial profiling - 174
Rand, Paul, Senator - 63
ratification - 16, 19, 31, 61, 85, 129, 130, 121, 141, 142,
227, 228, 234, 236, 237, 238, 225, 269, 271
ratified - 6, 9, 13, 17, 55, 88, 89, 123, 129, 193, 197, 200,
202, 204, 211, 213, 214, 218, 221, 226, 227, 228, 229, 231,
234, 236, 238, 241, 243, 247, 251, 254, 256
rebellion - 72, 207, 208, 209, 250
receipts and expenditures - 77
receiving the funds - 52
recession - 8, 56, 57
reconsideration - 49
records - 16, 25, 119, 120, 174
redress of grievances - 155, 163, 164
regulate - 7, 8, 10, 53, 55, 57, 65, 165, 168
regulate the value - 7, 55, 78
regulation of Congress - 76
regulations - 40, 53, 54, 114, 115, 125, 152, 168, 179, 245
religion - 4, 127, 155, 156, 158, 159, 160
religious test - 139, 140
removal - 27, 40, 92, 93, 94, 95, 96, 97, 107, 207, 208, 245,
246, 251

305

signers of the Constitution - 143, 144
silver - 78, 79
Sinems, Kyrsten, Congresswoman - 100
six years - 33, 219, 317
slave - 27, 28, 29, 62, 71, 122, 123, 132, 204, 206, 207, 209
slaveholders - 210
slave owners - 28, 122, 123
slave states - 29
slavery - 9, 27, 28, 29, 71, 72, 122, 123, 125, 137, 203, 218
smear campaign - 89
social caring - 22
social media - 100
society - 3, 114, 156, 163, 164, 178, 185, 189, 193, 317
socio-economic - 174
soldier - 5, 167
sound bites - 87, 220, 221
South - 28, 132, 213
South Carolina - 27, 144, 179, 195
Southern States - 29, 71, 72, 205, 210
sovereign - 194
sovereign immunity - 196
sovereignty - 9
sovereign entities - 194, 258
Speaker of the House - 33, 94, 246, 248, 249
special interest groups - 32
specific individuals - 20
speech - 45, 47, 155, 158, 161, 162
speeding - 262, 264
spend money on anything it wants to - 77
spending - 34, 35, 52, 77, 223, 224
standard of weights and measures - 55, 58
standing army - 66
state government - 13, 16, 33, 99, 126, 130, 149, 221
State of the Union - 104, 105, 125

T

under the authority of the United States - 47, 135, 136, 137
underground railroad - 123
uniform - 21, 25, 50, 54
Uniform Code of Military Justice (UCMJ) - 11
uninformed people - 89
United Nations - 63
United States - 6, 8, 9, 17, 19, 20, 21, 23, 25, 26, 33, 36, 37,
38, 40, 44, 45, 46, 47, 49, 50, 51, 52, 53, 54, 55, 58, 66, 67,
69, 70, 74, 78, 79, 80, 83, 84, 87, 89, 90, 91, 95, 98, 99, 100,
101, 102, 103, 105, 106, 107, 108, 109, 110, 111, 112, 116,
117, 124, 125, 126, 131, 135, 136, 137, 139, 141, 145, 175,
185, 191, 193, 195, 199, 200, 201, 205, 206, 207, 208, 209,
210, 213, 216, 219, 220, 224, 227, 229, 235, 239, 243, 253,
269, 270
United States of America - 2, 17, 19, 73, 83, 105, 141, 158
United States v Pink (1942) - 138, 271
United States v Sprague (1931) - 131
universities - 73, 161
unlawful imprisonment - 72
unlimited debt - 221
unlimited war - 63
unreasonable searches - 5, 171
unreasonable seizures - 5, 171
upside down - 67
urban - 89, 124
US v Lanza (1922) - 178
useful arts - 59

V

vacancies - 33, 35, 36, 104, 226
value - 7, 9, 27, 28, 55, 57, 99, 132, 185, 186
value of money - 7, 8, 57

vessels - 64, 76
vested - 23, 69, 83, 107, 108, 109, 146
vested rights - 146
veteran - 11
veto - 49, 50
vice-president - 15, 36, 37, 42, 83, 85, 87, 88, 89, 90, 91, 92,
93, 94, 95, 106, 199, 200, 207, 208, 231, 232, 233, 234, 239,
243, 245, 246, 247, 248, 249, 250
victim - 62, 186, 188, 189, 262
victimless crime - 262, 264
video - 32
vile - 162
vindictive - 102
violate - 3, 61, 78, 100, 136, 137, 139, 145, 150, 153, 161,
162, 172, 175, 268
violated - 26, 31, 55, 78, 103, 108, 171, 194, 259, 268
violating - 139, 153, 162, 178, 213, 271
violation - 6, 51, 57, 103, 107, 108, 112, 189, 193, 215, 218,
235, 263, 264, 265
Virginia - 166, 259
viscous - 162
vote - 6, 24, 25, 28, 33, 36, 42, 44, 49, 50, 84, 85, 86, 87, 90,
199, 200, 201, 207, 208, 209, 213, 229, 239, 243, 247, 250,
253, 255, 256
voter fraud - 213

W

war - 5, 9, 45, 46, 61, 62, 63, 64, 80, 81, 116, 117, 167, 177,
210, 223
war on drugs - 46
war-chest - 102
warden - 72

311

Z

1

5

$500 billion - 218
5,000 - 32
50,000 - 6, 7, 31
501(c)(3) - 156, 157, 158, 159

6

60 vote rule - 37, 42
60,000 - 7
61 votes - 42

7

700,000 - 31
750,000 - 174
760,000 - 240

8

800,000 - 7

About the Author

He has been actively engaged in Economics for fifty-six years with an Undergraduate degree in 1965 and a Master's degree in 1972. He completed his Doctorate in Political Economics in 2016. In the late 1960s he observed the creation of the two-tiered international gold standard resulting in the abolishment of the international gold standard in 1971. He then also observed the follow-on interest rate and inflation explosion of the 1970s.

He has followed the shadow government since the 1960s and has read hundreds of thousands of pages concerning politics and economics and their relationships over these fifty-nine years. He began writing in 2005 and produced a political newsletter every Tuesday for six years, from 2006 to 2012.

He has completed a six volume set, *Liberty: Will it Survive the 21st Century,* comprising over 2,200 pages. The set presents the problems of government in our current society along with solutions. In addition, he has written a basic economics for home schooling and another for everyday use. Both of these two books addresses economics in a manner that is easy to understand.

He began The Provis Institute of Political Economics in January 2016 to award undergraduate and graduate degrees in Economics. This institute was established to provide an avenue for students to achieve an education within their financial capabilities that teaches practical economics for everyday life. The website can be found at ProvisInstitute.com.